Sparking Student Creativity

PRACTICAL WAYS TO PROMOTE INNOVATIVE THINKING AND PROBLEM SOLVING

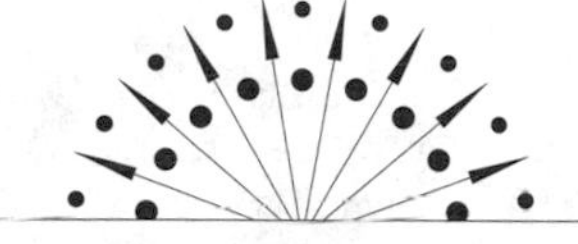

Sparking Student Creativity

PRACTICAL WAYS TO PROMOTE INNOVATIVE THINKING AND PROBLEM SOLVING

Patti Drapeau

Alexandria, Virginia USA

1703 N. Beauregard St. • Alexandria, VA 22311-1714 USA
Phone: 800-933-2723 or 703-578-9600 • Fax: 703-575-5400
Website: www.ascd.org • E-mail: member@ascd.org
Author guidelines: www.ascd.org/write

Judy Seltz, *Executive Director;* Richard Papale, *Acting Chief Program Development Officer;* Stefani Roth, *Interim Publisher;* Julie Houtz, *Director, Book Editing & Production;* Lorraine Sobson, *Editor;* Ernesto Yermoli, *Project Manager;* Thomas Lytle, *Senior Graphic Designer;* Mike Kalyan, *Manager, Production Services;* Valerie Younkin, *Production Designer*

PAPERBACK ISBN: 978-1-4166-1935-2 ASCD product # 115007

Quantity discounts: 10–49, 10%; 50+, 15%; 1,000+, special discounts (e-mail programteam@ascd.org or call 800-933-2723, ext. 5773, or 703-575-5773). Also available in e-book formats. For desk copies, go to www.ascd.org/deskcopy.

ASCD Member Book No. F15-1 (September 2014 PSI+). ASCD Member Books mail to Premium (P), Select (S), and Institutional Plus (I+) members on this schedule: Jan, PSI+; Feb, P; Apr, PSI+; May, P; Jul, PSI+; Aug, P; Sep, PSI+; Nov, PSI+; Dec, P. For current details on membership, see www.ascd.org/membership.

Library of Congress Cataloging-in-Publication Data

Drapeau, Patti.

Sparking student creativity : practical ways to promote innovative thinking and problem solving / Patti Drapeau.

pages cm

Includes bibliographical references and index.

ISBN 978-1-4166-1935-2 (pbk. : alk. paper) 1. Creative thinking—Study and teaching. 2. Creative ability in children. 3. Critical thinking—Study and teaching. I. Title.

LB1062.D68 2014

370.15'7—dc23

2014018287

23 22 21 20 19 18 17 16 15 14 1 2 3 4 5 6 7 8 9 10 11 12

· Sparking · Student Creativity

PRACTICAL WAYS TO PROMOTE INNOVATIVE THINKING AND PROBLEM SOLVING

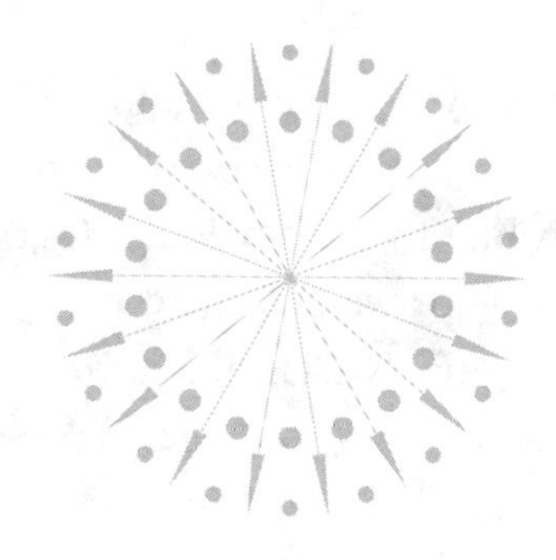

Acknowledgments

Thank you to Lenny Drapeau, first and foremost, for supporting me in all of my work projects. I always know you are there for me. You are my creative spark. I'd like to thank Sara Drapeau Bodi for calling me on her way home from school and for listening to me talk, almost daily, about this book, chapter by chapter. I'd like to thank Kip Bodi, Kasey Drapeau D'Amato, and Steve D'Amato, who all model a "can-do" attitude; you inspire me to push forward. I'd like to acknowledge Sandy Gerber; everyone needs a personal cheerleader and you are mine. I'd like to thank Lenore Burokoff, who continues to remind me the value of love and family.

I am fortunate to teach at the University of Southern Maine, where I have met so many wonderful graduate students who have shared such great ideas with me. They inspire me in more ways than they will ever know. I'd like to thank Lee Worcester, my colleague at the Maine Department of Education. She is always willing to listen to my ideas and offer suggestions in such a thoughtful way. I'd like to thank Diane Heacox for her friendship. It is wonderful to have someone to talk shop with who gets it. I'd also like to acknowledge Ourania En Baslis, my Australian colleague, who awakens my creative spirit.

I'd like to recognize Meg Bratsch, who convinced me there was a need for this book. I am grateful to the ASCD staff, especially Stefani Roth, who believed in the book and made it happen. I'd like to acknowledge the reviewers who helped drive the direction of this book. I am thankful for my editor, Lorraine Sobson, who said she wasn't creative but took on this book project anyway. Her editing skills helped to make this book what it is. Thank you, too, the reader, for acknowledging the importance of creativity in schools and making a difference.

Preface

I wrote this book for three very specific reasons: to help teachers reach more students, especially those who are disengaged in school and do not find what we teach interesting; to suggest strategies and tools that encourage creative thinking and creative products; and to show teachers how to intentionally use creativity in their classrooms. Some students have interesting ideas but are unable to express them because many of our instructional activities do not lend themselves to such ways of thinking. It is my hope that the tools and strategies presented in this book provide teachers with tangible ways to promote creativity—resulting in an increase in student achievement and love of learning.

Through creativity, we can reach more of the learners more of the time. Creative thinking can be integrated into any content area. This book brings together research, theory, practical applications, and current thoughts about the role of creativity in education. In writing this book, I reflected on all that I have read and learned, combined this with my own practical experiences, and translated the result into practice. This book also includes what I have learned about creativity from other educators who have shared their thoughts and ideas with me.

Consider a teacher who, as part of her master's program in gifted education, learns about the four creative thinking skill areas: fluency, flexibility, originality, and elaboration (Torrance, 1987a). She does not think of herself as particularly creative, so she is happy to learn some concrete ways to use creativity in her lessons. The more creative thinking skill lessons she presents, the more she grows to believe in her own creative ability. A year later, she takes the Torrance Tests of Creative Thinking (Torrance, 1987b). She realizes that the test assesses all four areas of creativity, so she makes sure her responses reflect fluency, flexibility, originality, and elaboration. Her score comes back in the 99th percentile.

Would the teacher have done as well on the test if she never learned about creative thinking skills and never practiced them with her students? This teacher doubts it; she feels quite certain the information she received and the practice she did with her students made a difference. I can state this definitively, because I am that teacher. This is my story, and it was the beginning of my pursuit of knowledge in the field of creativity. This experience taught me that if I can learn to be more creative, so can my students.

I encourage you to conduct creative thinking lessons even if you think you are not creative. Actually, it is really not about whether you are creative or not but whether you want to teach more creatively and are willing to try new ideas. *Sparking Student Creativity* will provide you with a rationale as to why creativity in education is important and with tools and strategies to help you make creativity intentional in your classroom. This book includes a "road map to creativity" that begins with the classroom environment and moves along four roads: one focusing on thinking-skill verbs and phrases, another on strategies, a third on innovation and creative problem solving, and a fourth on products. The book includes 40 "grab and go" strategies, aligns creativity lessons with standards, suggests different ways to design creative lessons, and shows how you can redirect lessons to promote creative thinking. This book is a practical resource that will guide you in your efforts to promote creativity in your classroom. I hope the ideas presented in this book will help you unlock your students' creativity, will serve to motivate your students, and will result in an increase in their performance and achievement.

Intentional Creativity

Fostering Student Creativity from Potential to Performance

Teachers and administrators throughout this country are focused on ensuring that both students and schools make adequate yearly progress and show growth. We order new textbooks, address curricula, concentrate professional development efforts on ways to increase student achievement, investigate new strategies to enhance students' academic progress and improve their behavior, and meet throughout the year in our professional learning communities to discuss what is and is not working. We do everything right.

However, at the end of many an academic year, schools see negligible improvements in achievement scores. Many students still act out and do not care about school. Teachers become disillusioned. Administrators face both low-performing, unmotivated students and disheartened staff. Do we need a miracle?

Perhaps it is simply that the scripted lessons teachers use are not motivating students. Veering from the scripted lesson—asking questions that promote critical and creative thinking, encouraging students to use divergent thinking to generate ideas to analyze and evaluate—might just be the key to changing students' attitudes and enhancing achievement. What many classrooms seem to be missing is *creativity*: creatively questioning to spark student inquiry and "hooking" student interest by using unusual images; asking students to connect content to unrelated ideas; and fostering hands-on, small-group, problem-based learning. What would happen if all teachers encouraged students to think creatively and produce creative products? Could this be the "miracle" we seek?

The idea that our educational system could use an infusion of creativity is one that has garnered much attention in recent years (e.g., Bronson & Merryman, 2010). Sir Ken Robinson's YouTube video *Do Schools Kill Creativity?* (2007) has had over 5 million video hits. Teachers are reading up on the basics of creativity (e.g., Beghetto & Kaufman, 2013) and watching videos that compare traditional lessons to those that require creative thinking (e.g., Ali, 2011; Maine Department of Education, 2013). Still, many educators feel that a piece is missing: precisely how to "teach" creativity and incorporate creative thinking in their classrooms. What does creativity look like, and how can schools foster it?

Creative instruction can be used to promote achievement across content areas, establish long-term learning (Woolfolk, 2007, as cited in Beghetto & Kaufman, 2010), encourage creative thinking and problem solving (Treffinger, 2008), and foster motivation and engagement. Creative thinking lessons build on critical thinking and go beyond simple recall to consider "what if" possibilities and incorporate real-life problem solving; they require students to use both divergent and convergent thinking. As Robinson has noted, "Creativity is not only about generating ideas; it involves making judgments about them. The creative process includes elaborating on the initial ideas, testing and refining them and even rejecting them" (2011, Chapter 6).

In a classroom that promotes creativity, students are grouped for specific purposes, rather than randomly, and are offered controlled product choices that make sense in the content area. Creative lesson components are not just feel-good activities. They are activities that directly address critical content, target specific standards, and require thoughtful products that allow students to show what they know. In the creative classroom, teachers encourage students to become independent learners by using strategies such as the gradual release of responsibility model (Fisher & Frey, 2008).

Creativity is not just for low-performing schools; using creative strategies and techniques helps all students think deeply and improve achievement. Creativity is not only for disengaged learners; it is motivating for all learners. Creativity is not just for students in the arts; it is for students in all classrooms in all content areas. Creativity is not just for high-achieving students; it supports struggling students and those with special needs as well. Creative thinking is not just for those students who are good at creative thinking; it is for all students. Promoting creativity in the classroom is not just for some teachers but for all teachers.

Exploring the Creativity Concept

Just what is creativity? Although creativity is often synonymous with having original ideas, definitions of the word differ. Whereas Robinson defined *creativity* as "a process of having original ideas that have value" (Azzam, 2009, p. 22), Gardner felt that creativity as a human endeavor does not have to be novel or of value (1989). Amabile (1989) defined a view of creativity as having expertise in a field along with a high level of divergent skills. And although some researchers hypothesize that creativity is separate from intelligence, others claim a relationship between creativity scores and IQ scores (Kim, 2005).

In addition, perceptions of creativity reflect cultural differences. Westerners generally think of creativity as novelty and emphasize unconventionality, inquisitiveness, imagination, humor, and freedom (Murdock & Ganim, 1993; Sternberg, 1985). Easterners, on the other hand, think of creativity as rediscovery and emphasize moral goodness, societal contributions, and connections between old and new knowledge (Niu & Sternberg, 2002; Rudowicz & Hui, 1997; Rudowicz & Yue, 2000). Both cultures value product creativity (Kaufman & Lan, 2012).

From a practitioner's point of view, although creative thinking is not defined solely by divergent thinking, it is associated with divergent thinking—and divergent thinking can be taught. *Divergent thinking* requires students to think of many different ideas, as opposed to *convergent thinking*, when there is only one right idea. Both are necessary for creativity: a student uses divergent thinking to generate different solutions to a problem or challenge and then uses convergent thinking to decide which one will provide the best results.

Students need to know and understand what creativity is so that they target their responses appropriately. Creativity is not just about elaborate products; it is also a way of thinking. When students hear the teacher say, "I want you to use creative thinking when you...," they should know that the teacher is looking for many ideas, different kinds of ideas, detailed ideas, or possibly a one-of-a-kind idea. Shared vocabulary and meanings are important if teachers want creativity to work.

Understanding Characteristics of Creative Students

Csikszentmihalyi (1996) described two types of creative people: "big C" creative people, those who are eminent in their field or domain and whose work often leads to change, and "little c" people, who use their creativity to affect their everyday lives. Many students do not think of themselves as creative; they believe that creativity is beyond their reach and think creativity is something that very few people engage in. They think creativity is only about big C people or students who excel in the arts. When students realize they don't have to be a big C person to be creative, then creativity becomes accessible to them. As a result of this newfound realization, students feel less pressure to come up with a one-of-a-kind idea and become willing to engage in day-to-day creative thinking activities and undertake creative products. They create realistic expectations about themselves regarding their ability to produce creatively. The more students are willing to use creative thinking, the more engaged they become.

Creative lessons instill excitement and interest, and as students become more engaged, they put out more effort. Dweck (2006) noted that students who have a *fixed mindset* do not believe effort and engagement make a difference; they believe they are born with a certain potential and it does not change, so they "are always in danger of being measured by failure" (p. 29). Students with a *growth mindset*, on the other hand, believe their skills and abilities can be developed. These students engage in hard work and demonstrate effort. When they make mistakes, they learn and grow from them. Students with a growth mindset are much more likely to use creativity as a source of engagement.

Creativity can be viewed as a cognitive style or preference: just as some students prefer to think critically, using analytical or evaluative thinking, and others prefer to use factual knowledge, certain students are inclined cognitively toward creative thinking and problem solving. In addition to differentiating instruction on the basis of student ability, interest, or learning profile (see Tomlinson, 1999), teachers also can differentiate lessons based on students' preferred cognitive style. Teachers might assign creativity activities to students who prefer to think creatively or, better yet, may group together some students who prefer creative thinking with those who prefer critical thinking.

An 8th grade social studies teacher I know was encountering behavior problems with one of her classes. She began to dread teaching this class and constantly struggled to find activities to engage the students. After asking students to rate themselves on a scale from 1 to 10 based on the characteristics of creative thinkers (see below), she found that 80 percent of the class considered themselves creative. This information was interesting to the students and very helpful to the teacher. She changed her lessons to emphasize creative thinking and creative products, and her discipline and management problems disappeared.

Students Who Think Creatively...

- Express ideas other students don't think of.
- Like to choose their own way of demonstrating understanding.
- Ask questions that may seem off-topic or silly.
- Enjoy open-ended assignments.
- Prefer to discuss ideas rather than facts.
- Prefer to try new ways of approaching a problem rather than accepted ways.

Creating the Classroom Climate

The starting point in the creative learning experience is the classroom and the classroom environment. Basic conditions of a creative learning classroom include providing a safe environment, supporting unusual ideas, providing choice, utilizing creative strategies and techniques, encouraging multiple solutions, incorporating novelty, and providing constructive feedback (Drapeau, 2011, p. 30). Students who learn in a creative environment, are exposed to creative activities and assignments, and observe their teacher modeling creative thinking will become more creative thinkers (Sternberg & Williams, 1996). A creative learning environment that embraces students and engagement along with critical thinking and creative thinking skills is essential to student achievement (Boykin & Noguera, 2011, 2012; Marks, 2000, as cited in Jensen, 2013).

The creation of a truly creative learning environment is deliberate. Teachers who want to see significant effects from their use of creative teaching strategies (i.e., enhanced thinking and creative processing) must make teaching creativity intentional and explicit (Higgins, Hall, Baumfield, & Moseley, 2005). In many classrooms, teachers introduce or review content but spend little time specifically naming the thinking process, describing what the process entails, or providing students with feedback as to how to improve. Their use of pure discovery and unguided instructional approaches is significantly less effective and less efficient than instructional approaches that place a strong emphasis on guiding student learning (Beghetto & Kaufman, 2010; Kirschner, Sweller, & Clark, 2006). Thus, in order to make thinking-skill instruction explicit, teachers guide student learning by naming the thinking skill in the lesson, describing how to do it well, and providing students with feedback that helps students think creatively about the content.

In the creative classroom, students recognize the relationship between the content they are studying and how they think about the content (Anderson et al., 2000). For example, when students brainstorm reasons for immigration laws, they need to know not only about immigration laws but also what *brainstorming* means, and how to do it well. Rubrics or feedback tools (see Chapter 7) are essential for assessing both students' content knowledge and their creative thinking skills. Using these tools also helps students see that thinking creatively about the content is as valued as content knowledge.

Unveiling the Creativity Road Map

The first stop on the road to achievement is to identify the nonnegotiables. The nonnegotiables consist of the curricular standards, the required content, and the skills that are the target of a lesson (Drapeau, 2004). Then, the teacher chooses one of four roads on the Creativity Road Map (see Figure 1.1) or combines roads to intentionally integrate creative instruction with content.

Road I: Targeting Creative Thinking Verbs

On Creativity Road 1, the focus is on creative thinking verbs and verb phrases. To promote creative thinking in the classroom, teachers pay attention to the verb in the questions they ask. Asking students to "describe the relationship between the heart and the circulation system and share the description in a paragraph" does not promote creative thinking; the verb *describe* directs students to merely recall known ideas. Utilizing creative thinking verbs, on the other hand, accesses creative thinking. On Creativity Road 1, teachers use verbs that encourage multiple answers, different kinds of answers, unusual answers, or elaborative answers (e.g., *brainstorm, generate, connect, relate, design, create, produce, construct, elaborate, embellish, predict, improve*).

For example, instead of asking students to describe the relationship between the heart and circulatory system, a teacher asks students to brainstorm all the many different types of relationships that exist between the heart and circulatory system. The thinking focus of this activity is on the creative thinking verb *brainstorm*. Students are expected not only to generate known ideas but also to stretch their thinking to include new ideas and possibilities. Creativity Road 1 is a good starting point for teachers who are just beginning to use creativity in their classrooms.

FIGURE 1.1

The Creativity Road Map

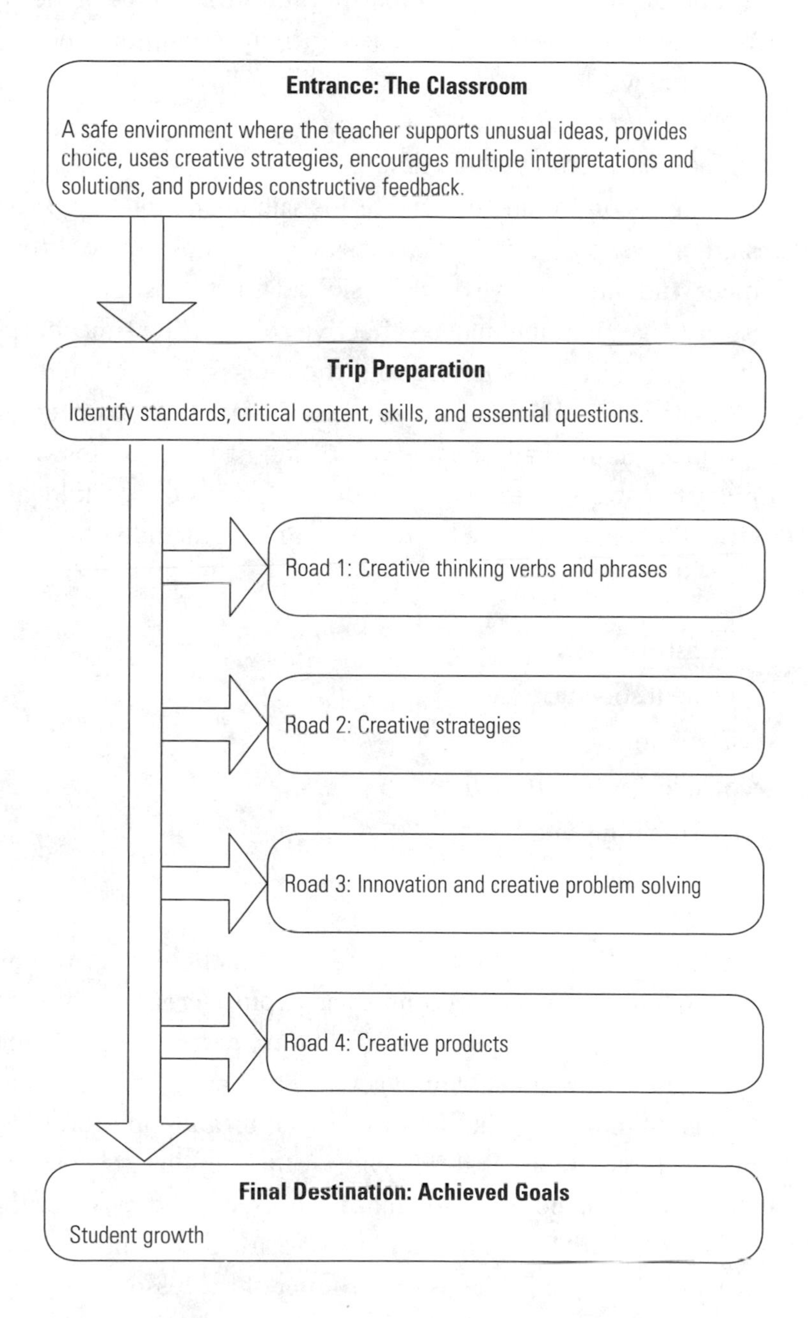

However, it is just the beginning of the journey; creativity in the classroom requires more than substituting verbs or a verb phrase ("Grab and Go" Idea #1, Chapter 2). Interaction, sparking of ideas, and additional strategies are needed to help students produce truly creative work.

Road 2: Focusing on Creative Strategies

The second road to creative instruction is to design (or redesign) a lesson by using an instructional strategy or tool that enhances students' creative thinking skills. Direct questioning that fosters creative thinking may be effective some of the time, but a steady diet of direct questioning and whole-class instruction does not promote interaction and engagement. Instructional strategies that promote more than one answer, different kinds of answers, or unusual answers often require group activities to spark ideas. Activities that are conducive to creative thinking include

- webbing,
- brainstorming,
- problem solving,
- visualizing,
- considering points of view,
- transforming, and
- symbolizing.

The 40 "grab and go" strategies in this book help teachers of all grade levels and content areas explore creative content instruction. For the lesson on the circulatory system, the teacher could enhance the brainstorming activity by having students use the "What Stands for What" strategy ("Grab and Go" Idea #8, Chapter 2) to create an abstract symbol that represents circulation. The symbol is not the product of the lesson; rather, it serves as a prewriting tool for students to use before generating a paragraph about the topic (which is the product of the lesson).

Road 3: Using Creative Processes

Creativity Road 3 focuses on creative thinking in the procedures and processes that students use when they are focusing on creative problem solving and innovation. These processes follow certain steps that may or may not include creative activities but always include creative thinking. For example, in the circulation lesson, small groups of students might use the creative problem solving model (Isaksen & Treffinger, 1985; see discussion in Chapter 6) to explore the topic. They begin by thinking of the different problems people might encounter when dealing with a circulatory medical condition. Once students identify a specific underlying problem, they brainstorm different solutions and then determine the best solution for the underlying problem. This is one example of a step-by-step process that encourages creativity.

Road 4: Applying Creative Products

Creativity Road 4 focuses on creative products. Creative products can be simple or sophisticated; they allow for a variety of different responses through multiple modalities (e.g., written, kinesthetic, visual, verbal) and may incorporate technology. For example, a literature unit might include a digital storytelling component (see University of Houston Education, 2014), encouraging students to think outside the box to elaborate upon characters, settings, stories, and insights by creating multimedia presentations on websites such as StoryBird and Animoto. For the circulation lesson, students could create PowerPoint presentations, posters, or a multimedia presentation (e.g., using Glogster) to illustrate their identification of a particular problem and how they addressed it. Creative products may be shared with the class, the school, the community, or the global community. They can be small-scale projects, but they can just as easily be multifaceted, long-term projects that involve people from diverse locations.

Utilizing Multiple Roads

When trying to go from one place to another, we often take more than one road. This is also true with instruction. Teachers may decide to use one or more roads in a lesson. The teacher who decides to use a creative thinking verb (Road 1) in a prompt also engages students in a creative thinking strategy (Road 2) when they are working through the creative problem solving process (Road 3). The lesson culminates in a creative product (Road 4). The Creativity Road Map helps teachers intentionally control the type and degree of creativity that occurs in the lesson.

Making Creativity a Habit

Brain research helps us to understand how to improve our creative thinking and make creative thinking a habit. The creative drive is a result of the interaction between the frontal lobe (where we generate ideas), the temporal lobe (where we judge), and the release of dopamine (which makes us feel good). Learning creates neural pathways in the brain, which are reinforced with use. Our brains prefer patterns, predictions, success, emotion, and meaning. "If there is no emotional or intellectual connection to new information... it will be discarded and attention will be withdrawn" (Willis, 2006, p. 44). Creative thinking, however, requires establishing new pathways and generating new and unusual ideas, which is "contrary to the brain's native leanings" (DiSalvo, 2011, Chapter 1). By practicing creative thinking, students become comfortable making new, meaningful connections and thinking of new possibilities rather than relying on established neural pathways. With enough practice, this new way of thinking becomes habitual and automatic.

Our brains are wired for success, which means students like to be assured of an outcome where there is only one answer: the right answer. This is not what creativity is about. With creative thinking, as long as students can defend their reasoning, many answers can be correct. To be able to grow in creativity and fully engage in creative lessons—to be able to make creativity a habit—students need to be able to trust the process.

Students will make it a habit to express their creativity in an environment where they feel encouraged to do so. In the creative learning classroom, both teacher and students are sensitive to diverse needs and respectful of others' thinking and self-expression. Creativity will not become a habit in a classroom where students are afraid of failure or making mistakes, overly focused on grades or worried about being different, or where they experience rejection, criticism, or bullying. Making creativity a habit, making a difference in student's performance and self-esteem, is only possible when students use creative thinking consistently and continually while engaged in authentic tasks with meaningful content in a safe environment.

Reflecting on and Extending Chapter Information

1. Why is it important to make creativity intentional?
2. Creativity is not just about the product; it is a way of thinking. What does this mean to you?
3. What type of creativity is already happening in your classroom? How can you tell if your creativity instruction is making a difference?
4. Do you know which students in your classroom are more creative than others? How is this information useful to you?
5. What does your vision of a creative classroom look like and sound like?

Practical Creativity

Making It Work in the Classroom

Creativity is infectious; if you want to become more creative, surround yourself with creative people and seek out creative environments. Like mastering anything else, if you practice creative thinking, you will get better at it. The same goes for your students: practicing creativity will help students extend their thinking beyond the status quo. But to encourage students to become more creative, we must first consider how the teacher makes a difference.

Results of research on creativity and the work of creativity theorists provide teachers with tips on how to promote and nurture student creativity (Figure 2.1). These include elements specific to the classroom environment, students' thinking-skill development, and teaching strategies and approaches.

Exploring the Teacher's Role

The teacher's role is to develop a classroom environment that embraces creativity. Pannels and Claxton (2008) noted that *climate* (for our purposes, the classroom) affects creativity, and Piirto (2004) observed that "creativity demands emotional risk taking" (p. 417). Therefore, the teacher provides an emotionally **safe environment** where students feel free to share thoughts and ideas. Students in the creative classroom also understand the value of representing their ideas in different ways. They are comfortable asking questions that are unusual and challenge the status quo because they have been encouraged to make new connections that go beyond the "right" answer. The teacher supports creativity by encouraging unusual ideas and provides positive feedback verbally and nonverbally. Modeling appropriate responses to creative ideas is essential in building students' understanding of what is and is not acceptable in this particular classroom. All of these elements are part of a secure teacher-student relationship, which promotes student achievement (Hattie, 2011).

FIGURE 2.1

Nurturing Student Creativity

Provide students with ...	Interesting work Challenging work Realistic goals and time frames
Help students ...	Understand that creativity can create a feeling of disequilibrium Embrace anxiety and fear about generating "what if" possibilities
Support students by ...	Integrating creative thinking skills Scaffolding instruction rather than "rescuing" students Coaching and facilitating discussion Providing constructive feedback Differentiating instruction
Establish an environment that ...	Values different types of creativity Values teamwork Is emotionally safe and positive

The teacher uses **novelty** to spark attention in a creative environment. Lessons that promote curiosity, suspense, and interest engage students and enhance learning (Koutstaal et al., 1997, as cited in Willis, 2006). Brain research provides evidence that novelty excites the brain. When teachers provide new materials or new resources or utilize new strategies, the brain wakes up and pays attention. Some ways that teachers can provide novelty include dressing up as a story character or a figure in history, using props and real artifacts, playing background music, telling jokes, rearranging the furniture, playing games to review, and changing the flow of a lesson.

In a creative climate, teachers provide students with **choice** as often as possible. Choice is essential to creativity (Sprenger, 2010) and is motivating because it gives students a sense of control over their learning, resulting in a feeling of empowerment. Choice reinforces the teacher-student relationship by acknowledging individuality (Deci, 1995). Choice does not have to be totally open-ended to be effective; although it can be completely student-initiated (e.g., students identify a product to illustrate understanding), it can be as simple as providing two or three options for a culminating product.

The teacher knows that a **sense of community** is essential in the creative classroom; by continually re-forming groups, the class develops a sense of community and students learn to value each other's individual strengths and abilities. Although whole-group instruction may be effective in certain situations, small groups are relevant when promoting creativity because creativity is deeply social (Farrell, 2001; John-Steiner, 2000; Sawyer, 2003, 2006b); Sawyer noted that "creative insights typically emerge from collaborative teams and creative circles" (Sawyer, 2006a, p. 42). Different types of small-group instruction include the following:

- *Ability groups*, based upon student ability in a specific content area (as opposed to tracking students),... consider students' ability to achieve in a specific content area and are not based on students' ability to think creatively. Ability groups are generally fixed, although they do not have to be; students should be able to move from one group to another if their ability changes.

- *Cooperative groups* are based upon student interest, or they may be formed randomly and comprise students of different ability levels. Often, students take on specific roles within the cooperative group. The emphasis of this type of grouping is on both academic and social learning and rarely takes into account cognitive preferences.
- *Flexible groups* are formed and re-formed according to individual needs, strengths, and preferences. When the focus of the group changes, so do the members in the group. This type of grouping enables a supportive creative environment.

The classroom teacher provides interesting and challenging work for students and sets **realistic goals and time frames** to help students be successful. Csikszentmihalyi (1996) identified the state of intense engagement and complete absorption as "flow"; when students are engaged in flow, they lose track of time. Although there are not many opportunities for students to reach this state of being in a school setting, teachers should still strive to foster conditions that allow for flow to occur.

In the creative classroom, students need to feel comfortable generating many different possible solutions and answers rather than seeking a single "right" answer. The more ideas students generate, the more likely some of these will be creative (Simonton, 1999). When students practice brainstorming they learn to tolerate ambiguity. Providing **scaffolding supports** (and then gradually removing them), rather than rescuing students from frustration, encourages students to generate divergent ideas that are ambiguous. Students will also need support in developing their creative thinking skills, because the creative process can cause angst; as animator Chuck Jones observed, "Fear is vital in any creative work [and] anxiety is the handmaiden of creativity" (Goleman, Kaufman, & Ray, 1992, p. 44). Scaffolding support systems should enable students and promote autonomy, rather than fostering students' dependence on the teacher.

Coaching students, particularly with setting measurable goals and breaking down processes into discrete steps, can help them develop intrinsic motivation, which influences creativity (Amabile, 1998). Teachers in creative classrooms serve as coaches when they provide students with resources, modeling, and advising, and develop criteria for measuring progress and success. Coaching students may also extend to competitions, but this type of coaching only influences intrinsic motivation when the competitions promote teamwork, creativity, and feedback (e.g., Odyssey of the Mind, Destination Imagination, Future Problem Solving, Exploravision).

Targeting Creativity Skills

Paul Torrance, commonly known as the "father of creativity," identified four creative thinking skills (1987a). His research provides evidence that these four skills can be taught and assessed (see Chapter 7):

- *Fluency.* The ability to generate many ideas focuses on the key word *many.*
- *Flexibility.* The ability to generate different kinds of ideas focuses on the key word *change.*
- *Originality.* The ability to generate a one-of-a-kind idea focuses on the key word *unusual.*
- *Elaboration.* The ability to add detail or extend ideas focuses on the key phrase *add on.*

In the creative classroom—where students are asked to brainstorm many (fluency), different (flexibility), and unusual (originality) ideas; add to an idea (elaboration); or combine it with another idea (flexibility)—these four skills can and generally do overlap.

Fluency

The target of creative fluency is not to generate a single outstanding idea but to generate many ideas. Quantity is the goal; through quantity, we hope to find some quality responses. Most often, teachers use some sort of brainstorming technique with students to encourage creative fluency. Students can brainstorm orally or silently (by writing responses and passing their papers around for others to add ideas). In "stop and start" brainstorming, students brainstorm ideas, stop and evaluate ideas, and brainstorm again. If students are good at brainstorming, then their ability to be creative may be specific to their ability as a fluent thinker. If they are not good at brainstorming, they can improve with practice.

Every teacher has encountered students who seem challenged by a brainstorming activity. Students who know the content information only at a surface level often have difficulty generating many ideas about the topic because they have limited knowledge. Some students have the knowledge but are just weak at brainstorming. Strategies teachers can use to help students having difficulty brainstorming include the following:

- *Use the classroom environment as inspiration.* Tell students to look around the room when they are stuck and can't think of any ideas. Is there something in the room that they can associate with the content information? For example, if students are brainstorming a list of everything they know about tsunamis, noticing that the sun is shining outside may be a reminder that a tsunami can occur during a sunny day.
- *Use students' interests to help them generate ideas.* If the brainstorming activity surrounds why a literary character behaves a particular way, encourage students to associate the behavior

with the similar behavior of a character in their favorite book, a television show, or a sports person in the news.

Students who do not develop creative fluency will generally rely on the first idea that comes to mind—which is often a common idea, rather than one that demonstrates deep thinking about the content. In addition to improving their fluency in generating multiple answers, students generate a variety of "correct" responses. For example, if students are asked about the types of things people might have found on the Oregon Trail during the Westward Movement, "a computer" is not a correct response; answers must make sense within the parameters of the question. The better the parameters of the question are defined, the more relevant students' responses will be.

Flexibility

For students to be able to think more deeply about content, they need to be able to think of problems and situations in different ways. Students demonstrate flexible thinking when they consider different points of view, when they make analogies and metaphors, and when they suggest changes or improvements.

To be able to use flexible thinking, students must know and understand the content beyond a surface level. As with fluency, students may need practice and direction to learn to generate many *different* ideas. A student who generates many ideas is using fluent thinking, but does not demonstrate flexibility if all of the ideas focus on the same kind of ideas. When teaching students to use flexible thinking, it is important to stress the expectation for students to generate not just many responses but different kinds of responses.

Students who understand the content well may still be unable to generate different kinds of ideas; this indicates that they require additional practice with their flexible thinking skills.

Practice helps, but the teacher must serve as a coach and teach students strategies they can use when they run out of ideas. One way to coach students is to help them understand that different kinds of ideas fall into different categories. For example, the teacher calls out a category, "animals," and students list many animals. Before long, the teacher calls out "food." The students switch gears and start listing foods. This continues until the students not only understand but feel what it is like to bounce their ideas from one category to another. Once students grasp this, we can ask them to use flexible thinking whenever we want students to change something. For example, "How might the story be different if Cinderella was not poor?" or "What are many different ways the South could have won the Civil War?" By thinking in categories, students presumably will not get stuck in one-track thinking.

Another way to help students become "unstuck" in their thinking is to model forced association. For example, a teacher can ask students how a slogan such as "slow and steady wins the race" applies in many, varied ways to the story of Cinderella, or to the concept of an electrical circuit, or to mathematical problem solving. This strategy demonstrates how flexible thinking helps us to make connections.

Years ago, Alex Osborn identified specific types of questions that could be used to evoke flexible thinking (1963). Eberle's SCAMPER mnemonic (1971)—substitute, combine, adapt, modify/maximize/minimize, put to other uses, eliminate, and rearrange—built on this concept. Figure 2.2 illustrates how a 4th grade teacher in Maine used SCAMPER to promote students' flexible thinking during a unit on their home state's industry, resources, foods, and economy; the teacher used the official state treat of Maine to hook student interest. The students used the mnemonic to discuss what, if anything, was changed, substituted, combined, adapted, and so on, to transform common chocolate cake into Maine's famous dessert, whoopie pie.

FIGURE 2.2

Flexible Thinking Using SCAMPER Questioning

SCAMPER Skill	Question Prompt	Student Product
Substitute	What would happen if you substituted vanilla for chocolate?	List possibilities, then select one to illustrate
Combine	What would happen if you combined chocolate cake with whipped cream?	List possibilities, then select one to illustrate
Adapt	How can you change the shape of a round cake?	List possibilities, then select one to describe
Maximize or minimize	What might the largest or smallest piece of chocolate cake look like?	List possibilities, then select one to describe
Put to another use	What are other uses for chocolate cake?	List possibilities
Eliminate	What would happen if you left out the sugar from a chocolate cake?	Describe ideas
Rearrange or reverse	What would it be like if chocolate cake were considered a healthy snack?	List possibilities

Originality

Originality is the ability to generate a one-of-a-kind idea. Many students need to develop their fluency and flexibility skills before they can generate original ideas. The focus on fluency as a starting point helps in the development of originality; if a student generates many ideas, then it is more likely that one or two ideas will be unlike any other student's ideas (Simonton, 1999). Flexible thinking enables students to compare their own ideas to see how different they are from one another; an idea that is unlike any of their other ideas can be considered the original idea, for this student in this lesson.

It is important for students to understand that coming up with an original idea is contextual. It is based on a certain lesson, at a certain point in time, in certain circumstances. Students may be able to come up with original ideas in some situations and not in others. As when teaching fluency and flexible thinking, it is important to explicitly discuss the process of original thinking with students. For example, a lesson that asks students to brainstorm a list of ways to solve the problem of world hunger (fluency), then to categorize their individual ideas to see how many different kinds of ideas they generated (flexibility), and then to identify whether they have any unique (original) ideas illustrates the process conceptually for students. (This particular approach follows the Talents Unlimited Thinking Skills Model; Schlichter, 1986.)

As when teaching students to use flexible thinking, it can be helpful to incorporate students' current interests and popular cultural references when encouraging originality. One middle-school social studies teacher I know adapted his usual unit on Maine to incorporate original thinking. He designed a webquest that included many fluent and flexible thinking activities. Students could choose the form for their summative assessment: participate in Maine Idol (modeled after *American Idol*) or create a PowerPoint presentation. Students researched information about the state's different counties on the web, and then small groups of students wrote songs (set to popular tunes) distilling the information or created PowerPoint presentations. The project was very popular with students and enabled the teacher to assess both student mastery of the content and the originality of their products.

Often when teachers think of originality, they think of original products or inventions. This is fine, except that we want to also value original thinking. The "grab and go" ideas at the end of this chapter include ways to target original thinking.

Elaboration

Elaboration is the ability to add details to another's idea or extend an idea—to take an idea and "run with it." Like other creative thinking skills, divergent thinking requires students to have a firm grasp of content in order to expand on a topic, concept, issue, or theme. When introducing the concept of elaboration as a creative thinking skill, provide students with examples of elaboration in the world (e.g., computers, housing renovations, sequels to movies or classic works of literature, scientific concepts or theories, organizations developed to respond to a concern or problem in the community). Help students to understand the difference between quality elaboration, as compared to simply adding details or repeating an idea in a different way; this is just more of the same. One way to do this is to have students compare writing pieces (e.g., one that is long yet does not say much with a shorter piece that actually provides more elaboration).

As with originality, elaboration skills build on fluency and flexibility; as students become more comfortable generating many and different ideas, they will also be able to identify those ideas best suited to expanding or elaborating. It can help to scaffold instruction of elaboration by providing students with templates, specific resources, or tools such as graphic organizers to help them manage information and organize their thinking.

What happens when the teacher wants the student to elaborate and the student responds with one or two more sentences that are not elaborative? This is an indicator that the student is lacking in content knowledge or is simply unable to think of additional responses. Encouraging students to "piggyback" on each other's ideas will model for them the process of elaboration. For example, if one student says a tsunami causes an unusually high tide, another student might piggyback on this idea by observing that a tsunami often causes erosion; the first student's comment about a high tide made the next student think about the tide washing away the sand and soil.

Assessing Creativity

Creativity can be assessed as part of either formative or summative assessments; the assessment, however, needs to include criteria specific to creative thinking (see Chapter 7 for more on this topic). If students are instructed to think of many ways to change the ending of a story, then they should be assessed on how many ways they are able to change the ending of the story while maintaining the integrity of the original story. Other criteria may specify that the ideas make sense or address the quality of the responses. Student learning is guided by comprehensive rubrics that reflect all components of a lesson: the content, the thinking process required, and the product.

A good rubric not only lets students know what the teacher expects but also provides a means of self-assessment so students can identify their strengths and weaknesses. The rubric should include varying levels of performance to assist students in setting goals for future performance. This type of rubric also reinforces student autonomy: once students "understand what to do and why, most students develop a feeling that they have control over their learning" (Brookhart, 2008, p. 2).

Figure 2.3 is a sample of a rubric developed to assess creative fluency. The assignment was for students to list many ways to change the ending of a story, while maintaining the integrity of the original plot. They also were to write a descriptive paragraph elaborating on the story, including one of the new story endings. The rubric's clarity enables students to understand the expectations of the assignment. There are two parts to this assignment: brainstorming alternate endings to a story, and producing a descriptive paragraph extending the reading. Although it targets fluency, the assignment contains elements of flexibility (generating different kinds of ideas) and originality (expressing original ideas), while also addressing writing standards (organization, clarity of expression, no grammar or spelling mistakes).

FIGURE 2.3

Sample Rubric to Assess Creative Fluency

List many ways to change the ending of the story (while maintaining the integrity of the original plot) and write a descriptive paragraph elaborating on the story that includes one of the new story endings.

Skill Component	1	2	3	4
Content	Does not understand the text or story	Can retell main points	Understands text components and includes details	Understands text composition, transitions, and tone and includes many details
Fluency	Lists 1 or 2 ideas for alternate ending	Lists 3 or 4 ideas for alternate ending	Lists 5 or 6 ideas for alternate ending	Lists more than 6 ideas for alternate ending
Connection between original text and new ideas	Most of the ideas are not logical or do not make sense contextually	Few of the ideas are logical and make sense contextually	Some of the ideas are logical and make sense contextually	All of the ideas are logical and make sense contextually
Descriptive paragraph (product)	Paragraph is poorly organized and unclear and includes grammar/spelling errors	Paragraph is mostly well organized and includes few grammar/spelling errors	Paragraph is well organized and clearly written, with no grammar or spelling mistakes	Paragraph is well organized and clearly written, contains no mistakes, and expresses original ideas

Students can brainstorm individually, although, as I have noted previously, brainstorming in groups encourages more ideas and usually results in greater creativity. If the brainstorming for an assignment such as this is undertaken in small groups, either do not assess the fluency or conduct a group assessment by counting the number of responses and giving either a small-group or a whole-class fluency score. This type of approach uses competition positively, in that students work together to achieve a goal. However, when assessing the group's performance, it is better to give descriptive feedback rather than translate the assessment into individual grades (see Chapter 7).

Creative thinking activities often do not exist in isolation but are incorporated within a bigger lesson. Whether creativity is a big part of the lesson or a small part of the lesson does not matter; what makes a difference is to start talking about creativity with students, use creativity to help students build understanding about the content, and provide students with descriptive feedback on the content, thinking process, and product of the lesson.

The 12 "grab and go" ideas presented at the end of this chapter include ways to support students in developing different creative thinking skills, ways to embed creative thinking skill development within existing lesson plans, and ways to integrate creative thinking within a larger teaching strategy. They are easy to implement, can be adapted for use in most content areas, are appropriate for a range of student learning needs and styles, and address students' ability to produce information rather than consume information. As noted in Chapter 1, it is important to explicitly teach creativity; that is, in addition to identifying the content knowledge being accessed or reinforced, specifically tell students that the lesson requires creative thinking, identify the creative thinking skill being used, and model the process for them.

Reflecting on and Extending Chapter Information

1. Why does creativity in particular need to be nurtured?
2. Why do we need to utilize creative strategies and techniques if we are already using effective teaching practices?

3. How important are grouping practices to successful creative thinking activities?
4. How does a student's level of independence affect creative performance?
5. Make a plan: choose three strategies to try this week. Which strategies will be the most effective with your content?

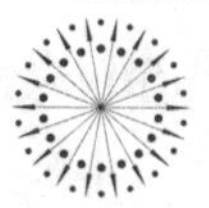

"Grab and Go" Idea #1

Starter Phrases

Starter phrases are useful when traveling on Creativity Road 1. They are easy to use, can be used to substitute for an existing verb, and can be used with simple or complex content.

If targeting *fluency*, use starter phrases such as the examples given here, and connect them to your content. Remember, a fluency prompt means the teacher is looking for *many responses*. Fluency starter phrases direct students to list or orally respond to the following:

- Situations in which something might occur
- Ways to do something
- Things that serve a similar purpose
- Other uses for an object or invention
- Things that come to mind when a word, person, or situation is mentioned
- Words that relate to the same object or concept
- Ways to express a similar idea
- New ways to do something
- Questions to ask about a new concept or information
- Consequences of a particular turn of events
- Words that describe an object or event

If targeting *flexibility*, the brainstorming activity becomes more specific and focused. Teachers are not just looking for many ideas; they are looking for varied types of ideas. Students are thinking about changes that occur as a result of their flexible thinking. Examples of flexibility starter phrases include the following:

- In what ways might...?
- List different ways to modify....
- What would happen if...?
- Describe many possible changes to....
- List different situations, topics, and so on, that....
- What are different ways to improve upon...?

If targeting *originality,* starter phrases encourage students to think of original or unusual responses. Adjectives such as *unique, original,* or *unusual* help students understand that the focus of the lesson is originality. Examples of originality starter phrases include the following:

- How might you design...?
- List ways to develop...
- Invent a...
- Make a one-of-a-kind...
- Devise your own way to...
- Propose a novel approach for...

If targeting *elaboration,* the starter phrases help students know to produce an elaborate response. Examples of elaboration starter phrases include the following:

- Add to...
- Build on...
- Expand on...
- Extend upon...
- Enhance by...

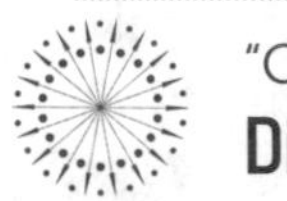

"Grab and Go" Idea #2

Diversify Questions

This "grab and go" idea primarily targets fluency, although the strategy is easily adapted to incorporate elements of flexibility, originality, and elaboration. This strategy reminds teachers to use different types of creative questioning and is an important strategy for teachers who are on Creativity Road 1.

Teachers can get stuck asking the same type of fluency questions. To jump-start students' use of creative thinking skills, present a variety of categories or things for them to consider. Use categories to help them diversify their questioning, but ensure that students don't just provide recall; they need to go beyond recall to infer, predict, and consider possibilities.

Sample fluency questions include the following:

- *What would happen if... ?* For example, what would happen if the British had won the Revolutionary War? What would happen if we did not have any form of measurement? What would happen if Edison had not pursued the invention of the lightbulb? What would happen if we had no judicial system?
- *Unusual uses.* For example, what are some unusual uses for a cell phone? What are some unusual uses for a car? What are some unusual uses for a condemned factory building? What are some unusual uses for a pet?
- *Product improvement.* List ways to improve the Declaration of Independence. List ways to improve weather forecasting tools. List ways to improve a website. List ways to improve food distribution.
- *Perspective taking.* List many different stakeholders and brainstorm ideas or opinions from their point of view. For example, describe how different characters respond to an occurrence in a fiction text, different people and their views about education, or different political systems.

- *Cause and effect.* For example, list different causes and effects of the Civil War. List causes and effects of a character's action in a fiction text. List causes and effects of not recycling.

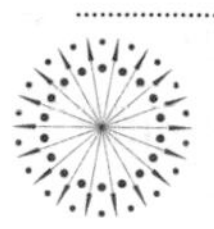

"Grab and Go" Idea #3

Reverse Brainstorming

Reverse brainstorming is a strategy placed on Creativity Road 2. With reverse brainstorming, students approach a problem from the opposite side. Students generate many ideas about the reverse of what they want. They reflect upon their answers to generate a new way of thinking about the original problem. This requires students to use both fluency and flexibility, teaches them to develop new viewpoints and perceptions about a problem, and promotes original solutions or responses. For example, reverse brainstorming ideas include the following:

- Increase pollution instead of reducing pollution.
- Promote more wars instead of thinking about how we can minimize war.
- Increase our consumption of water instead of thinking about how we can conserve water.
- Promote drug use instead of thinking about reducing drug use.
- Intensify a situation in a fictional text so that it is worse for a character instead of solving a problem.
- Aggravate an already bad situation instead of correcting a bad situation.
- Generate the worst ideas about a topic or situation instead of generating positive ideas.
- Study ineffectively instead of identifying study skills.

"Grab and Go" Idea #4

Sound Effects

This strategy is on Creativity Road 2 and is more complex than the preceding strategies. When targeting fluency, flexibility, or originality, focus student attention on listing many possible sound effects, different types of sound effects, and creating an original interpretation of text using sound effects. Begin the lesson by asking students to pay attention to sound effects in a video or audio piece. What purpose do sound effects serve? Do the sound effects help the listener understand the message of the piece? Assign text selections (fiction, news story, opinion piece) to small groups of students and have them brainstorm different sound effects that could be used to enhance the meaning of the text selection. The sound effects could be limited to available musical instruments or online resources—or no outside resources at all (e.g., clapping, stomping, verbal sound effects). Students then select the best effects to enhance understanding of the text selection. A worksheet (see Figure 2.4) can support students when using this strategy, helping them note which sound effects they are using and when. After organizing their information, they rehearse, then record or perform their pieces for the others in the class.

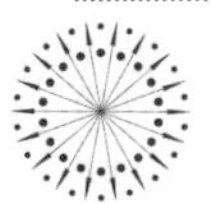

"Grab and Go" Idea #5

Trading Cards

The Trading Cards strategy, like most strategies, is on Creativity Road 2 (unless it is the actual product of the lesson, in which case it is Creativity Road 4). Creating trading cards allows students to distill and express content knowledge in a way that exercises their creative skills. The thinking skills that are emphasized in the Trading Cards activity are fluency and originality.

FIGURE 2.4

Reading with Sound Effects			
Student names:			
Title of text:		Performance date:	
List of possible sound effects:			
Type of sound effect	Page or paragraph number	"Word" when sound is added	Who makes the sound
1.			
2.			
3.			
4.			
5.			
6.			
7.			

For this hands-on activity, students cover the face of an actual trading or playing card and redesign the face to address content. Card faces can be designed from photographs, watercolor, collage, doodles, or mixed media and painted, glued, or drawn on the playing card. They may also be created on a computer (see ReadWriteThink, www.readwritethink.org/classroom-resources/student-interactives/trading-card-creator-30056.html). The card itself serves as a tool to motivate students to study a topic in depth, make concrete or abstract associations, draw conclusions, or predict future possibilities.

For example:

- In a 5th grade Greek mythology unit, students choose a Greek god or goddess and create a card symbolizing the traits of the Greek god or goddess. The symbols should be abstract rather than concrete. The assignment includes researching, generating many different symbols or statements, and selecting the most appropriate elements to include on the card. Originality is emphasized in students' choice of symbols and the two- or three-dimensional designs on the playing card itself.
- In a 4th grade class, students create mathematical playing cards illustrating what they know and understand about adding fractions with unlike denominators.
- In an 8th grade physical science class, students create cards for different astronomy concepts.
- In social studies, cards are used as culminating products in units to show conditions on the Oregon Trail or to demonstrate the political climate that existed during the signing of the Declaration of Independence.

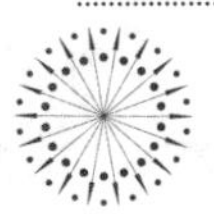

"Grab and Go" Idea #6

Connect and Solve

This activity, on Creativity Road 2, requires students to use both fluency and flexibility. Students exercise their flexible thinking skills by making connections or associations between the characteristics of a random word and a problem to solve or address.

First, the class as a whole generates a list of nouns. Then, small groups of students are each assigned a noun; this can be done by having a group representative pull a word slip out of a bowl or a sticky note off a board, or by having groups assign each other nouns. The small groups then generate as many connections as possible between their noun and the lesson topic. They use these ideas to find a way to solve a problem in a story, explicate issues surrounding a historical event, or resolve environmental problems. Groups choose which solution they think is best and present their findings to the class.

For example, in Louis Sachar's story *Holes* (1998), Stanley Yelnats is accused of stealing and sentenced to dig holes at Camp Green Lake juvenile detention center in Texas. After reading the story, students use the Connect and Solve strategy to determine the best way for Stanley to cope with his situation at the detention center. A student from each group chooses three nouns by pulling slips of paper out of a hat. The groups are to choose one noun (discarding the other two) and brainstorm characteristics about the noun, then relate the characteristics to the situation in the story and identify their best idea. One group chooses *dog, shoe,* and *book*. They choose *dog* and generate the following characteristics about dogs: *friendly, loyal, exercises, sleeps a lot, likes to eat,* and *playful*. Next, they make connections:

- *Friendly*: Stanley can dig holes with friends.
- *Loyal*: Stanley is loyal to his friends.
- *Exercises*: Stanley thinks of digging holes as his new get-in-shape program.
- *Sleeps and eats*: Stanley can sleep during breaks, and he likes to eat.
- *Playful*: Stanley makes a game out of digging holes.

The students decided their best idea for Stanley in his situation is to think of digging as his exercise program because it will help him get in shape, become stronger, and result in building his self-esteem. The groups of students share their responses with each other. Students discuss what a rewrite of the story might look like based upon their new ideas.

"Grab and Go" Idea #7

Change Matrix

The change matrix is a graphic organizer from Creativity Road 2 that helps guide students' flexible thinking, focusing on different ways to change ideas or improve something. To create the matrix, provide a list of descriptors and a prompt to which students must respond. Figure 2.5 illustrates how the matrix can be adapted for different content areas; when creating a change matrix, be sure that topics and descriptors match the intent of the lesson. For instance, in the science example, students would use knowledge gained from their study of clouds to talk about what the different changes in the cloud formations mean.

FIGURE 2.5

Change Matrix

Prompt	Descriptors			
Mathematics	Larger	Smaller	Longer	Shorter
Change in the dimensions of a quadrilateral...				
English Language Arts	Stronger	Weaker	Nicer	Braver
Change in the behavior or attitude of a character...				
Science	Bigger	Smaller	Brighter	Darker
Change in cloud formations...				
Social Studies	Greater	Lesser	Worse	Better
Change in the impact an explorer had...				

"Grab and Go" Idea #8
What Stands for What

This activity, where students create an abstract symbol or picture that is associated with the content, is based upon Wilhelm's symbolic representation concept (2002). It targets flexible thinking, which students need to be able to use in order to make connections between the symbol and the content, and also requires students to identify forced associations between a symbol and the content information. Like the other strategies, this activity is on Creativity Road 2.

For example, in a literacy lesson, a middle-school English teacher asked students to think of a symbol that represents the theme in the story *The Outsiders* by S. E. Hinton (1967). One student created a picture with a frame around it; the picture consisted of cut-out pieces of paper in the shape of people. Half of the picture showed people-shapes that were all the same size and color; this symbolized how people in the story wanted to be the same. On the other half of the picture, the people-shapes were different sizes and colors, symbolizing the idea that a variety of people are more interesting than when everyone is the same. The picture also had a frame with pieces of mirror stuck on it; names of places were written over the mirror pieces. The names symbolized the idea that no matter where you go, you are always you: you can't run away from yourself.

Making symbols to represent content is a powerful way for students to make meaning. At first, students might choose literal symbols to symbolize the content. In order to promote deep meaning, students need to explore unusual connections between symbols and the content. When they do make unusual connections, students explain the relationship between the symbol and the content and why the symbol is meaningful.

"Grab and Go" Idea #9

NUP

NUP stands for *new and unusual products* and resides on Creativity Road 4. This original thinking activity is suited to many content areas and can enhance existing culminating product or project assignments. When assigning a culminating project, focus student attention on creating something *new* (e.g., structure, item for the future, artwork, musical composition, shelter, solution, character).

This idea can also be adapted to requiring students to process information using three-dimensional materials. An example of using original thinking in a lesson to create a new and unusual product would be to provide students with a bag of diverse materials to devise props for a reenactment. The goal of this activity would be for students to use the materials in the reenactment in unusual and unique ways.

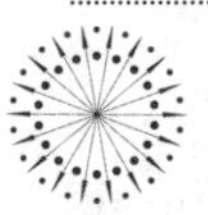

"Grab and Go" Idea #10

Be the Thing

Be the Thing is a Creativity Road 2 strategy that requires students to understand and apply personification. Students use fluent thinking to generate many responses and original thinking to place themselves in the role of an object. There are three questions to which students respond when "being the thing":

- How do you feel?
- What are your thoughts?
- What will you do?

This strategy is applicable to a variety of grade levels and content areas. Figure 2.6 illustrates how it has been used with an elementary class learning about parallelograms and a middle-school class reading Louis Sachar's *Holes* (1998). Most often teachers use this strategy as a prewriting technique; students use the ideas they generate to create a short description or a more elaborative writing piece. This strategy can also be used to generate a lively discussion designed to build deep meaning of the content.

FIGURE 2.6

Student Responses to "Be the Thing" Prompts

	"Be the Thing" Prompts		
Grade level and content area	**How do you feel?**	**What are your thoughts?**	**What will you do?**
Elementary school mathematics: parallelogram	Boxed in Structured I ippy	Will I ever straighten up? I depend on my opposite sides. I consist of smaller shapes.	I will let people manipulate me. I will be useful.
Middle-school English language arts: the shovel in *Holes* (Sachar, 1998)	Ashamed Sad Sore	I don't want to dig holes. I am ashamed I am used for this purpose. I am old and banged up.	I will break.

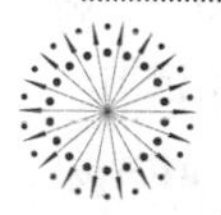

"Grab and Go" Idea #11

Lost and Found

In this Creativity Road 2 activity, students imagine finding some information that has been "lost." This imaginary lost information provides an elaboration or more detail about the known information.

For example, in an elementary science unit, students read the chapter "Flooding in Venice" in the book *Shaping Earth's Surface: Water* (Kramer, 2005). The teacher tells them to imagine finding an earlier draft of this chapter, which has additional information about the effects of the flooding that the author chose to leave out. What kind of information might this be? Students conduct research to find additional information appropriate for the chapter, write up this information in their own words, and then the class compiles it—enhancing both student content knowledge and their ability to work in cooperative groups.

This is a fun activity to do with students who are reading literature, too: tell students to imagine finding a whole chapter that is missing from their book. They must write a summary of this found information and place it in the appropriate place in the story in order to elaborate on the story without actually changing the plot.

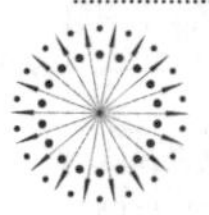

"Grab and Go" Idea #12

Many Voices

This activity, on Creativity Road 2, accesses students' flexible thinking and elaboration skills and can be easily integrated into a unit that typically generates opposing points of view. For example, students who are studying energy sources read about the different points of view surrounding strip mining. The teacher groups students and assigns them one of the points of view. Each student in the group writes a persuasive letter making a case for his or her viewpoint. Student groups trade papers, and each student highlights the most important statement in the letter. The group then works together to sequence the highlighted points. They read these sentences orally to the other group. Each person in the group reads one sentence.

"Many Voices" addresses many skills. First of all, students are elaborating on existing information about strip mining, not only by writing the letters but also when they talk in their small groups and identify their most important points. The group must work together to agree upon the order in which they will present their argument, which requires cooperation as well as a deep understanding of the content. Finally, they are presenting the opposite point of view. This helps them empathize more readily when discussing both points of view.

Creativity and the Common Core

Matching the "What" to the "How"

The Common Core State Standards (CCSS) provide rigorous targets for what we want students to know and understand. The standards provide an organizational system that addresses what to teach. The CCSS emphasis on text complexity, informational text, and critical thinking is intended to help students become more college and career ready. The CCSS defines content standards along with academic skills and understandings that provide an opportunity for students to learn challenging content.

Why not use creativity as a tool to help students in meeting the CCSS? As noted in Chapter 1, creative thinking skills can enhance student content mastery (see Beghetto & Kaufman, 2010), and the CCSS emphasis on text complexity would seem to require students to use both critical and creative thinking skills. However, a cursory review of the English language arts standards (National Governors Association Center for Best Practices, Council of Chief

State School Officers [NGA Center], 2010a) reveals that verbs associated with creativity are not emphasized; whereas the CCSS repeatedly uses verbs such as *recount, explain, cite,* and *summarize,* creative-thinking verbs such as *make connections, integrate,* and *infer* are used less often or not at all (at some grade levels). Similarly, the mathematics standards (NGA Center, 2010b) use *solve, apply, explain,* and *understand* much more frequently than the creative thinking verbs *interpret, extend,* or *compare.*

What this means is that teachers need to use their own elaboration skills to incorporate creativity when teaching to standards such as the CCSS. In order to integrate creativity, teachers need to be able to tweak their lesson plans so that they address critical thinking standards through the creative processing of information.

To illustrate how this can be done, consider the verbs *extend, compose,* and *generate.* A CCSS Grade 1 numbers and operations standard is for students to be able to "extend the counting sequence" (NGA Center, 2010b). An activity where the teacher asks students to extend the counting sequence 2, 4, 6, 8 does not encourage creative thinking; students can extend the sequence without necessarily extending their knowledge about patterns and sequencing. If, however, the teacher gives the students the sequence 1, 2, 3, 2, 1 and asks students to extend the sequence in as many ways as they can that make mathematical sense, then the teacher is asking students to extend the sequence *and* extend their thinking about sequencing. Students must use creative thinking to come up with multiple responses.

If teachers want to foster creative thinking, they must use their own imagination and creativity to integrate creative thinking skills into a lesson or refocus lessons to include these skills. This is not as difficult as it may sound; in addition to presenting information in ways that promote students' use of creative thinking skills (as illustrated in the math sequencing example), teachers can fairly easily deconstruct standards to see what they consist of and then "reconstruct" standards to incorporate creativity.

Deconstructing and Reconstructing Standards to Incorporate Creative Thinking

To deconstruct a standard, first identify the content, topics, subtopics, and concepts it contains; these are usually stated as nouns. Next, identify the verbs in the standard; the verbs target the thinking level (e.g., *describe, analyze, represent, determine*). One way to incorporate creativity into existing standards is to reconstruct the standard by replacing a verb with a creative thinking verb (Creativity Road 1); another is to modify or add qualifying words—adjectives and adverbs that describe to what degree the student is expected to respond.

For example (see Figure 3.1), a CCSS Grade 2 reading standard is to "identify the main topic of a multiparagraph text as well as the focus of specific paragraphs within the text" (RI.2.2; NGA Center, 2010a). The standard, in essence, requires students to know what a main topic is and what the focus of a paragraph is; students also must be familiar with the concept of multiparagraph texts. The verb *identify* is not just a low-level thinking verb; it is also not a very exciting verb. Reconstructing the standard to replace the verb with a creative thinking verb such as *substitute* results in a standard that promotes flexible creative thinking. The reconstructed standard now reads "substitute the main topic of a multiparagraph text as well as the focus on the specific paragraphs within the text." To respond to this prompt, students still need to be able to identify the original main topic and the focus in other paragraphs, but they will be thinking creatively when they make the substitutions. This sort of activity requires students to delve a bit deeper when thinking about the text and reinforces students' content understanding. In addition, it is more intellectually playful and challenging to make a substitution for a main topic than to simply identify the main topic. By changing the verb, the standard lends itself to fun and engagement; as mentioned in Chapter 1, engaging students this way can help them make meaning out of learning (Grant, Grant, & Gallate, 2012).

FIGURE 3.1

Reconstructing the CCSS: Using Creative Thinking Verbs

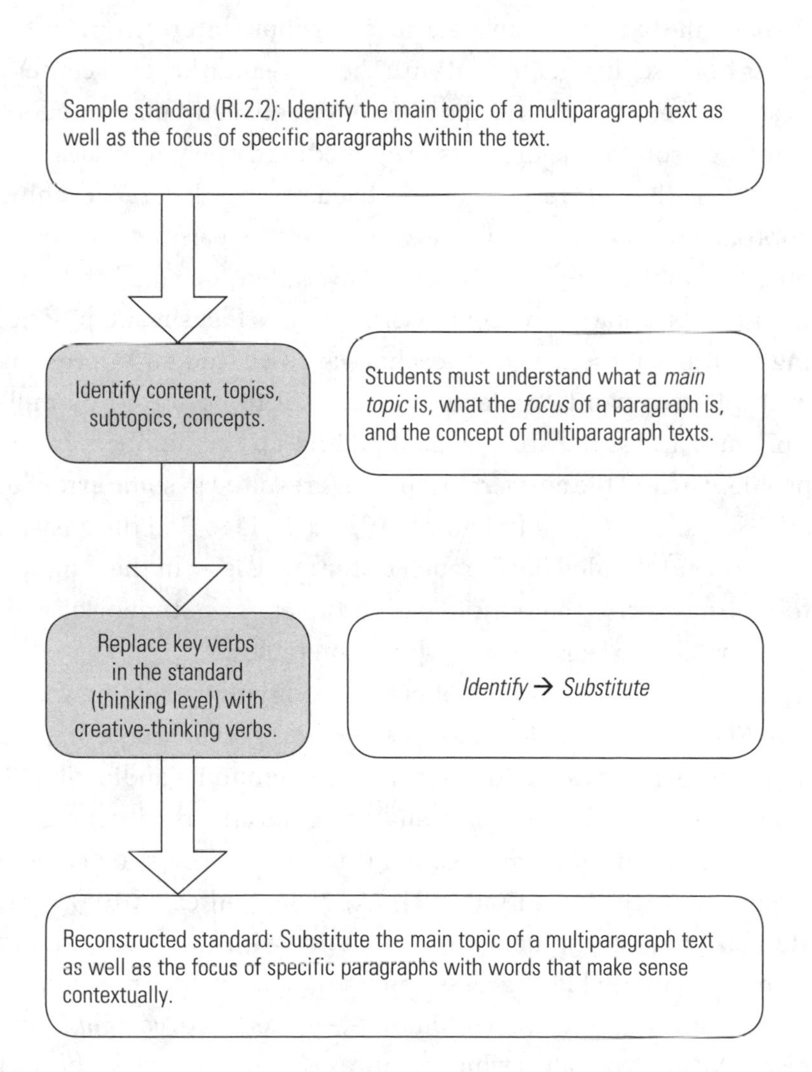

This may seem, at first glance, nonsensical. Why would a teacher ask students to make a substitution when they can't even identify the main topic? This type of a challenge can be intellectually motivating for students: if students want to make a substitution but don't know what to substitute because they can't identify the main topic, they now have a reason to learn what a main topic is. I call this "teaching through the back door." Instead of teaching the basics first and building to the complex, teaching through the back door can make learning more interesting for students because they get to deal with the more multifaceted content first. It's the same thing as the difference between a piano student learning a song at the first lesson and tediously playing scales.

A 4th grade teacher I know tried this "backward" teaching approach with a student who was resistant to learning the multiplication tables. Instead of having the student do computational worksheets and work on computer programs focusing on practicing multiplication facts, the teacher gave the student interesting multiple-step word problems that needed to be solved by multiplying. At first the student kept adding up the numbers in the problem to find the answer; this process resulted in some errors of addition and took the student a very long time to find the answer. The student decided it was much faster and easier in the long run to just memorize the multiplication tables. The student discovered a reason to learn the multiplication tables.

To demonstrate the effect of modifying qualifying words (see Figure 3.2), consider this Grade 7 reading standard: "Compare and contrast a written story, drama, or poem to its audio, filmed, staged, or multimedia version, analyzing the effects of techniques unique to each medium (e.g., lighting, sound, color, or camera focus and angles in a film)" (RL.7.7; NGA Center, 2010a). This standard requires students to be familiar with the listed literary forms, and to be able to access and understand different versions, techniques, and media. The thinking-level verbs are *compare, contrast,* and *analyze*—all of which require critical thinking on the part

FIGURE 3.2

Reconstructing the CCSS: Adding Qualifying Words

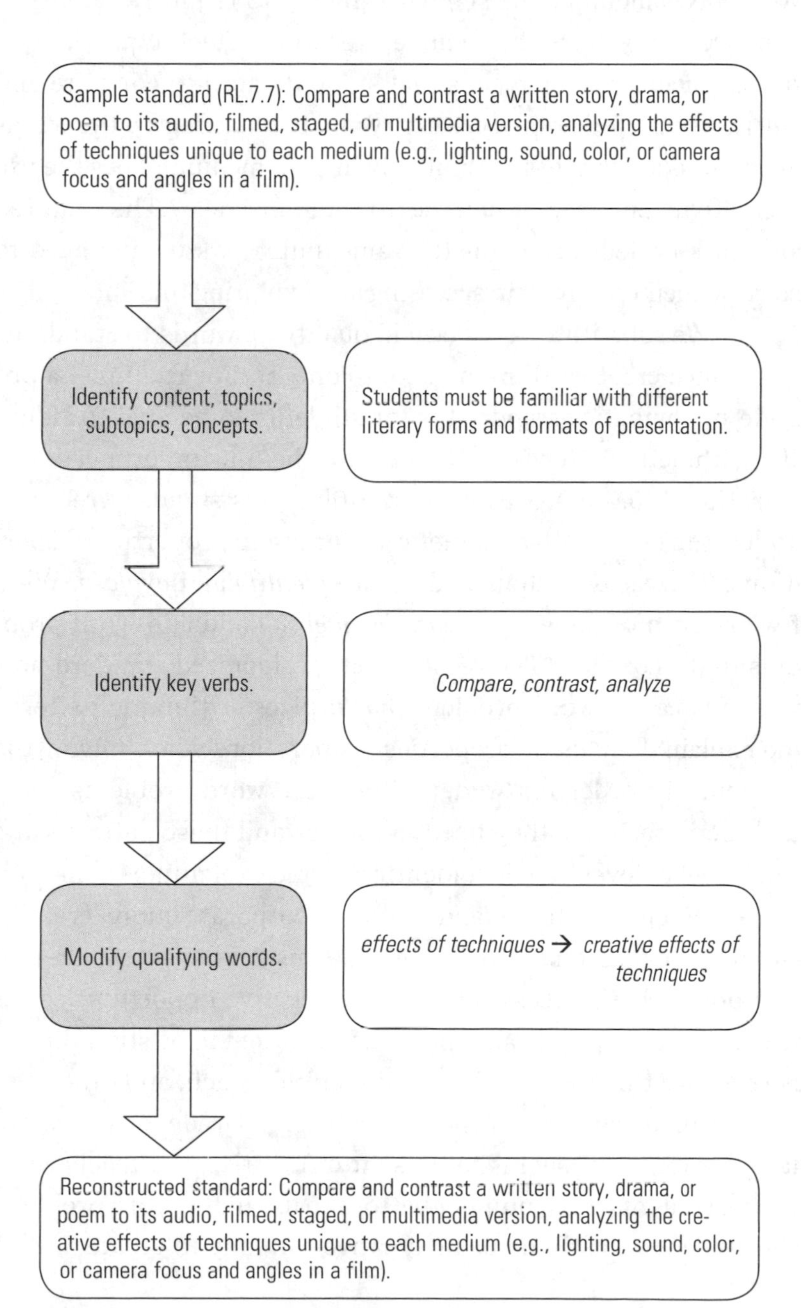

of students. In this case, it would be better to modify a qualifying word than one of the verbs. Adding the word *creative* before the word *effects* modifies the standard slightly to require students to compare and evaluate the creative effects of the techniques unique to each medium. This means that students need to compare and contrast both elements of creativity and to what degree the words and actions are expressed creatively in each medium: does the use of creativity enhance or detract from the message? The required content knowledge remains the same, but now students need to exercise their creativity in accessing and exploring this knowledge.

We substitute verbs or add qualifying words to standards to enhance creative thinking about content. For example, a 3rd grade mathematics standard is for students to be able to "identify arithmetic patterns… and explain them using properties of operations" (3.OA; NGA Center, 2010b). This standard requires students to know both arithmetic patterns and properties of operations. The verbs in the standard are *identify* and *explain*. What if we substitute the word *create* for *identify* and add word problems to the content? The reconstructed, enhanced standard now reads, "Create a word problem that utilizes arithmetic patterns and explain them using properties of operations when solving the problem." In order for students to create word problems using arithmetic patterns, they need to understand these patterns at a much deeper level than just identifying and explaining them.

When we alter standards to incorporate more creative thinking, we might have to differentiate instruction to ensure that all students have access to the same creative opportunities. As discussed in Chapter 2, any time students seem to be struggling to use creative thinking, teachers can scaffold, coach, and otherwise support their learning. If the reconstructed Grade 3 math standard, for example, seems to present difficulties, the teacher can tell the student which number pattern to use in the word problem. The student will still be using creative thinking to create a word problem, apply the arithmetic pattern, and explain it using properties of operations.

Targeting Creativity Thinking Skills with Standards-Based Activities

Another way to incorporate creative thinking in a standards-based environment is to take a typical lesson based on a standard and rework it to target a specific creative thinking skill. Figure 3.3 demonstrates how one standard can be addressed in four different ways, each targeting one of the four thinking skills. The figure shows examples of math and literacy standards from different grade levels and the creative thinking lessons that might be developed to help students access the standard. All of these lessons ask students to make meaning of content—by personalizing their associations with a topic (e.g., fog), using their own words to express a poet's message, considering a character's situation from a different perspective, or developing new ways to present or consider information. The lessons require students to extend their thinking beyond recall and rote repetition. Students still have to show or cite evidence, but the activities also incorporate choice, which is motivating for students and fosters creativity (Deci, 1995; Sprenger, 2010). Most of the lessons in Figure 3.3 focus on Creativity Road 1 because they target verbs or phrases rather than instructional strategies (Creativity Road 2), processes and procedures (Creativity Road 3), or products (Creativity Road 4).

Compare the creative thinking activities in Figure 3.3 with "typical" activities for the same standards:

- *For the 3rd grade literacy standard,* the typical approach would be to discuss (responding to teacher- and student-created questions) the important ideas in the book, and create a written response summarizing them.

FIGURE 3.3

Targeting Creativity Skill Areas with Standards-Based Activities

CCSS Key Ideas and Details	Target: Fluency	Target: Flexibility	Target: Originality	Target: Elaboration
Grade 3: Ask and answer questions to demonstrate understanding of a text, referring explicitly to the text as the basis for the answers. (RL.3.1) Text: *Sarah, Plain and Tall* (MacLachlan, 1985)	Small groups of students brainstorm and list all the situations in Sarah's life that prepared her for being a mother. They provide references to the text to support their ideas and create a graphic organizer.	Small groups of students discuss and list how the story would be different if Sarah were a mean mother. They provide references to the text where changes would occur in the storyline and how these would affect the overall story arc.	Small groups of students develop a contextually appropriate, unique process for finding a wife other than advertising. They provide references to the text where changes to the storyline would occur and discuss how these would affect the overall story arc.	Sarah was never married before and had no children of her own; in their groups, students discuss why taking on someone else's children could have been a challenge for her and develop written products elaborating on their ideas. They provide references to the text to support their ideas.
Grade 5: Quote accurately from a text when explaining what the text says explicitly and when drawing inferences from the text. (RL.5.1) Text: "Fog" (Sandburg, 1916)	Students brainstorm as a whole class all the things that fog reminds them of. They create written lists and compare and contrast their ideas to Sandburg's ideas about fog in a graphic organizer.	Students substitute *fog* with a different contextually appropriate thing the poem could describe. They rewrite the poem making the substitution.	Students create an original story, poem, or other product that represents fog using a dog rather than a cat. As a prewriting tool, students use a graphic organizer to compare and contrast their ideas to Sandburg's ideas about fog.	Students build upon Sandburg's description of fog by adding another stanza to the poem using elaborative language.

FIGURE 3.3 — (*continued*)

Targeting Creativity Skill Areas with Standards-Based Activities

CCSS Key Ideas and Details	Target: Fluency	Target: Flexibility	Target: Originality	Target: Elaboration
Grade 5: Use place value understanding to round decimals to any place. (5.NBT)	Students develop word problems that require rounding decimals. They choose from their list of word problems to create an easy, medium, and challenging story for their classmates to solve.	Students combine word problems that use fractions with word problems that require rounding decimals to create new word problems. They create easy, medium, and challenging problems for their classmates to solve.	Students invent a math game that requires players to round decimals. They create questions at easy, medium, and challenging levels.	Students are given rounding decimals word problems. They are to add useless and useful information. Other students determine which additional information is the red herring.
High school: Create equations that describe numbers or relationships: Create equations in two or more variables to represent relationships between quantities; graph equations on coordinate axes with labels and scales. (HSA-CED.A.2)	Students generate a list of consequences of not knowing how to graph equations with two or more variables. They produce a 2-minute video explaining why we need to know the relationship between quantities with two or more variables and how to graph them.	Students generate a list of consequences of substituting a 2-dimensional graph for a 3-dimensional graph to use with equations with two or more variables. Students produce a 2-minute video explaining what would happen if this substitution were to occur.	Students develop a unique way to show how a 2-dimensional graph can be used to represent equations with two or more variables. Students produce a 2-minute video that incorporates this interpretation and explains why we need to know the relationship between quantities with two or more variables and how to graph them.	Students enhance a 2-dimensional graph used to represent equations with two or more variables. Students produce a 2-minute video showing how the enhanced graph works best.

FIGURE 3.3 — (*continued*)

Targeting Creativity Skill Areas with Standards-Based Activities

CCSS Key Ideas and Details	Target: Fluency	Target: Flexibility	Target: Originality	Target: Elaboration
High school: Cite strong and thorough textual evidence to support analysis of what the text says explicitly as well as inferences drawn from the text, including determining where the text leaves matters uncertain. (RL.12.1) Text: Keats's quote from "Ode on a Grecian Urn": "Beauty is truth, truth beauty,—that is all / Ye know on earth, and all ye need to know."	Students develop a list of questions they would like to ask Keats about this quote. They cite examples from the text to support their ideas.	Students rewrite the quote by substituting certain words to make it more meaningful to them. They cite textual evidence to support their interpretation.	Students create an object with quotes and figures on it that tell a story. They create a list citing textual evidence to support their creation and indicate areas where their object reflects uncertain matters in the text.	Students elaborate on different meanings of the quote based upon different points of view. They cite textual evidence to support their ideas.

Note. CCSS = Common Core State Standards (National Governors Association Center for Best Practices, Council of Chief State School Officers, 2010a, 2010b).

- *For the 5th grade literacy standard,* students usually select a line from the poem and write a response as to the poet's intent.
- *For the 5th grade math standard,* students would complete a worksheet requiring them to round decimal numbers.
- *For the high school math standard,* students would graph equations on a handout, then create equations with two or more variables that fall between the equations in the handout and graph these as well.
- *For the high school literacy standard,* students typically would analyze the poem, particularly as to inferring information about the urn. They might use a graphic organizer to summarize this information visually.

The two "grab and go" ideas at the end of this chapter differ from those in Chapter 2 because they are designed to help teachers exercise their own creative thinking. The first "grab and go" idea is an exercise in comparing typical and creative lessons for different grade levels and standards; teachers identify the creative intent of the lesson. The second "grab and go" idea is a tool that provides an opportunity for planning, self-assessment, and reflection.

Reflecting on and Extending Chapter Information

1. The creative thinking lessons seem harder than the typical lessons. Are these lessons realistic for struggling students or English-language learners? Why or why not?
2. Teachers worry about preparing their students for standardized or performance-based tests. If the standards emphasize

critical thinking, is the use of creative thinking activities and lessons a waste of time? Why or why not?

3. Revamping lessons takes time. Is the time spent on redesigning activities and lessons worth it? Why or why not?
4. Teachers feel uneasy reconstructing standards because students are being tested on the original standards. How can teachers be reassured that this is okay to do?
5. Reconstructing a standard primarily focuses on Creativity Road 1. When teachers leave the standard alone they generally use creativity strategies and products (Creativity Roads 2, 3, and 4) to address the content in the standard. How do teachers know when to reconstruct and when to leave the standard alone?

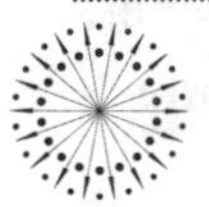

"Grab and Go" Idea #13

Typical vs. Creative Activities

Figure 3.4 is intended to help you visualize the relationship between the standard, the typical activity, and the creative activity for three different grade-level standards. The exercise is to identify whether a creative element is the *intent* of the lesson. Is the emphasis of the lesson on the creative thinking process and/or the creative thinking product? The first example is completed for you.

See if you can identify the creativity elements in the other two activities. Now, add some of your own typical activities and see if you can intentionally make them more creative. List three activities that you plan to do with your students. Change one activity to foster creative thinking. Change one activity to foster a creative product. Change one activity to foster both creative thinking and a creative product.

FIGURE 3.4

Comparing Typical vs. Creative Thinking Skill Lessons

CCSS Key Ideas and Details		Typical Lesson		Lesson Targeting Creative Thinking	
Cite the textual evidence that most strongly supports an analysis of what the text says explicitly as well as inferences drawn from the text. (RL.8.1)		Students analyze ideas that are communicated in Carl Sandburg's poem "Chicago" (1916) and select lines of text to support their analysis. Product: Written analysis		Students write an original poem using elaborative language about their hometown. They must maintain the same tone Sandburg uses in "Chicago," incorporating inferences from the poem. Product: Poem	
Creative thinking process?	Creative product?	Creative thinking process?	Creative product?	Creative thinking process?	Creative product?
No	No	No	No	Yes (elaboration)	Yes (original poem)
Understand that shapes in different categories (e.g., rhombuses, rectangles, and others) may share attributes (e.g., having four sides), and that the shared attributes can define a larger category (e.g., quadrilaterals). Recognize rhombuses, rectangles, and squares as examples of quadrilaterals, and draw examples of quadrilaterals that do not belong to any of these subcategories. (3.G.A.1)		Students draw rhombuses, rectangles, and squares, and cut and paste them in the correct category. They draw a quadrilateral that is not one of the three quadrilaterals listed and place it in the category "unknown." Product: Graphic organizer		Students draw quadrilaterals and create a picture by cutting and pasting them on a piece of paper. They may add other shapes to create the picture. They must use at least four different types of quadrilaterals, and must label the shapes. Product: Picture	
Creative thinking process?	Creative product?	Creative thinking process?	Creative product?	Creative thinking process?	Creative product?

FIGURE 3.4 — (*continued*)

Comparing Typical vs. Creative Thinking Skill Lessons

Weigh the possible outcomes of a decision by assigning probabilities to payoff values and finding expected values. (HSS-MD.B.5) Use probabilities to make fair decisions (e.g., drawing by lots, using a random number generator). (HSS-MD.B.6)		Students are told to suppose that their high school has decided to try same-sex math classes in an effort to raise math scores. Students research the number of same-sex math classes in the United States and determine if these classes are more successful. They make a scatter plot of the data and describe patterns, outliers, and positive and negative associations. They analyze the data and reported outcomes. They use probability to argue that the data either supports or refutes their school's decision. Product: Written report		Students create a hypothesis in their area of interest. They test their hypothesis using scatter plots and lines of best fit. They write a report using probability to evaluate the outcome of their hypothesis. They must support their thinking with evidence from their scatter plots and equations. Product: Written report	
Creative thinking process?	Creative product?	Creative thinking process?	Creative product?	Creative thinking process?	Creative product?
One of my typical activities:			How can I change this activity to foster creative thinking?		
One of my typical activities:			How can I change this activity to foster a creative product?		
One of my typical activities:			How can I change this activity to foster both creative thinking and a creative product?		

Note. CCSS = Common Core State Standards (National Governors Association Center for Best Practices, Council of Chief State School Officers, 2010a, 2010b).

"Grab and Go" Idea #14

Planning for Creativity

Figure 3.5 is a tool intended to help teachers to see if students use a variety of thinking skills in a unit, what creative products are in their unit, how many times they access the same Creativity Road, and if the creative lessons are distributed throughout the unit.

FIGURE 3.5

Creativity Planner	
Standard: Ex.: *Quote accurately from a text when explaining what the text says explicitly and when drawing inferences from the text.* *(CCSS, RL.5.1)*	Lesson or activity: Ex.: *Students build upon Carl Sandburg's description of fog (in "Fog," 1916) by adding another stanza to the poem using elaborative language.*
Creative thinking skill emphasized: Ex.: *Elaboration*	Creative product emphasized: Ex.: *None*
Creative road(s) emphasized: Ex.: *Creative Road 1 (thinking verbs and phrases)*	When in the lesson does this occur? Ex.: *Follow-up activity*
Standard:	Lesson or activity:
Creative thinking skill emphasized:	Creative product emphasized:
Creative road(s) emphasized:	When in the lesson does this occur?
Standard:	Lesson or activity:
Creative thinking skill emphasized:	Creative product emphasized:
Creative road(s) emphasized:	When in the lesson does this occur?

Note. CCSS = Common Core State Standards (National Governors Association Center for Best Practices, Council of Chief State School Officers, 2010a, 2010b).

Develop a creativity plan for your next unit of study. In the plan, identify the standard, the lesson or activity, the type of creative thinking skill emphasized (fluency, flexibility, originality, or elaboration), the creative product, what road or roads are being accessed (Creativity Road 1, 2, 3, or 4), and when this activity or lesson will occur. Figure 3.5 includes an example to guide your work.

Creativity and Imagination

Unlocking the Power of Imagination

As with *creativity*, the word *imagination* has been variously defined. McKim (1980) conceived of it as "all that you have ever learned or experienced: it is central to your every perception and act" (p. 88). In a 2008 taped presentation (Cornell University), Sir Ken Robinson described imagination as the process of bringing to mind "things that are not present to our senses." Milora (1987) explored the idea of imagination as the link between emotional and intellectual thinking: the images we imagine are created from the connection between what we feel and what we think, and aid in developing deeper understanding. Root-Bernstein and Root-Bernstein (2001) concurred with this idea, suggesting that "insight is born of emotions and images of many sorts conjured within the imagination" (p. 13).

Jazz musician Josh Linker observed that "the creative act is nonlinear" (Sawyer, 2013, p. 2); imagination is the spark that ignites creativity (Liu & Noppe-Brandon, 2009, 2010). Imagination is necessary if we are to make meaning of our experience. Imagination provides us with the ability to understand information and enables us to make sense of the world and the people in it. In the classroom, imagination enables students to explore new ways to think about ideas. Noppe-Brandon, Deasy, and Gitter (2011) gathered common threads about imagination from a variety of fields. Holzer's (2007, 2009) list of capacities for imaginative learning was supported in other findings (Michelli, Holzer, & Bevan, 2011): "noticing deeply, embodying, questioning, making connections, identifying patterns, exhibiting empathy, living with ambiguity, creating meaning, taking action, and reflecting/assessing" (p. 10). These capacities are integrated into the four conditions necessary for imagination to flourish: challenge, knowledge, environmental conditions, and motivation. Figure 4.1 illustrates how these conditions can be established in the creative classroom (Noppe-Brandon et al., 2011).

Establishing Conditions Necessary for Imaginative Thinking

Challenges, especially real-world challenges, invite students to use their imagination to extend thinking about what is known in order to solve real problems. By noticing, embracing, and questioning content, students begin to imagine possibilities. At one time, someone imagined a world where we could see the person on the other end of the telephone or hear a person talking on the television; at one time, someone imagined a printer typing out information or producing something three-dimensional; at one time, someone imagined robots doing surgery or computer glasses allowing doctors worldwide to assist with surgery. All of these things have evolved from embracing challenge—a figment of someone's imagination became a reality. The teacher in the creative classroom encourages imagination, freeing students to be intellectually playful.

FIGURE 4.1

Conditions That Support Imaginative Thinking	
Challenge	Ask students to • think individually or collaboratively; • come up with ideas beyond that which is known; • solve real-world problems; and • notice deeply, embodying information and questions.
Knowledge	Ask students to • access reproductive knowledge, • recall factual information, • access productive knowledge, and • form concepts through connection making and pattern identification.
Environment	Encourage students to take risks by • helping them minimize their fear of failure; • showing them how to accept ambiguity; • giving feedback only, no grades, some of the time; and • modeling empathy.
Motivation	Foster intrinsic motivation by • encouraging meaning making, • turning ideas into action, and • assessing and reflecting.

For example, in a science unit on the environment, students are asked to imagine a world where food is grown without pesticides. In an energy unit, students imagine a world without gasoline-powered cars. In a book study group, students imagine how a character would feel if something did or did not happen. Students can imagine ways to solve problems in all content areas.

Tim Berra noted that "knowledge—our storehouse of experience and information—is the raw material of imagination" (Noppe-Brandon et al., 2011, p. 7). **Knowledge** is affected by memory: in order to be able to access knowledge, students must remember information. There are two types of imagination, *reproductive* and *productive*. Memory is affected by reproductive imagination; "images made by functional magnetic resonance imaging technology show that remembering and imagining sends blood to identical parts of the brain" (Long, 2010, p. 13). This suggests that students with poor memory skills may also have less ability to imagine, which could affect their ability to be successful in creative thinking lessons in school. When developing lessons incorporating creativity, consider the need to provide scaffolding for students who struggle with memory problems.

Knowledge is an important factor in productive imagination, which involves the formation of concepts. Students form concepts based upon their ability to process knowledge by making connections and identifying patterns. Productive imagination allows students to create products to show what they know. If students cannot imagine something, they cannot create it. For example, if the teacher asks students to create a multimedia poster and the student has never seen one before, the student cannot imagine what is required. This is why it is essential for teachers to provide examples, models, and visuals to support student understanding.

The **environment** that fosters imagination also pushes the status quo; the environment allows for a safe place for risk taking, which means being able to accept failure. In order to make risk taking comfortable for students, teachers talk about the benefits of trying, making mistakes, and failing. Teachers model empathy and foster an environment of acceptance. They encourage students to accept ambiguous ideas. It can help students to reflect on historical precedents for failing before ultimately succeeding (e.g., if Edison had never risked failure or had let failure stop him, he might not have invented the first commercially viable version of the electric lightbulb). For students, the fear of a low grade may stop them from taking a risk. One way to encourage safe risk taking is to provide only feedback, with no grade. Students also may be afraid to use their imagination to think of many possible answers. One way to minimize this is to allow students to collaborate rather than require them to come up with many ideas independently.

Motivation, "the drive to do something because it is interesting, challenging, and absorbing… is essential for high levels of creativity" (Pink, 2009, Chapter 2). Amabile, Conti, Coon, Lazenby, and Herron (1996) defined *task motivation* as both the students' attitude toward the task and understanding the purpose of the task. Students are motivated when they feel there is meaning behind what they are doing, which results in taking action. Doing something new motivates some students; working in a group motivates others. Some students are motivated working in a subject area they like or excel in; others are motivated by achievement. All students are motivated when they attach value to what they are doing and when they feel they can be successful. It is motivational to realize that ideas can be transformed from imagination to productivity.

Bridgeland, Dilulio, and Burke Morrison's (2006) interviews with over 450 high school dropouts found that disinterest in their classes and a lack of motivation were a contributing factor to many of these students leaving school. Seventy-one percent of the dropouts wanted teachers to make school more interesting. Deci (1995) has advocated an autonomous support theory, suggesting that teachers step out of the way so that students will be self-motivated. For this to happen, students need to understand what motivates them and teachers need to establish classroom conditions that incorporate student motivators. For example, a teacher can allow students who are motivated by music to listen to music on headphones while they are working. Students realize that music is motivational and can use this knowledge to self-regulate their learning.

Another thing that motivates students is for them to see the results of their effort. As discussed in Chapter 1, students with a fixed mindset (Dweck, 2006) feel they are not smart and they never will be, no matter how hard they try—or, conversely, may feel they are so smart that they don't have to extend much effort. Students with a growth mindset, however, know that effort pays off. They know that persistence counts and that effort will help them to overcome obstacles, and they learn from criticism rather than shrink away from it. Their achievement is a result of their autonomy and efficacy. When students realize that they can actually change their brain, change their IQ, and change their performance in school through effort and hard work, this is empowering and motivating for them.

To motivate students in the creative classroom,

- provide students with the right level of challenge;
- ensure students have the appropriate tools and learning skills, such as note taking, memory techniques, and comprehension and problem solving strategies;
- encourage effort;
- connect with students personally;
- give students or allow students to discover a reason why they want to learn the content;
- provide students with feedback and data about their progress; and
- let students progress at their own pace.

Utilizing Strategies and Techniques to Access Imagination

Although teachers sometimes think that being imaginative means generating ideas that are not related to content, accessing imagination is intended to deepen students' understanding of complex concepts. Imagination is "a form of playful analogical thinking that draws on previous experiences, but combines them in unusual ways, generating new patterns of meaning" (Sternberg, 1999, p. 217).

Author Ridley Pearson has spoken and written extensively about his craft. One of his tips to budding writers, "Show, don't tell" (2012), provides guidance for teachers who would like to creatively access student imagination in their classrooms. When teachers provide students with facts, they are *telling*. For example, the teacher tells students that ocean water causes weathering and erosion, and that ocean waves also contribute to the erosion. Another teacher presenting the same unit shows students a video about weathering and erosion and asks them to draw conclusions; students then conduct research to determine whether their conclusions are correct. Still another teacher asks students to imagine water and rough surf pounding the beach during a storm. At high tide, the water goes over the sea wall and begins to flood the streets. This happens storm after storm. The teacher asks students to imagine the long-term effects of this situation on the beach and the beachfront property that sits just beyond the sea wall. The students draw conclusions and research their conclusions to see if they are correct. The first teacher has only told students about the content, the second teacher has shown them what it means, and the third teacher has shown them how they can use their imaginations to make connections.

Many teachers utilize a version of Pearson's three-act structure for storytelling (2010) when they teach students about the beginning, middle, and end of a story. This structure can be used to help students access imagination, too, by showing them how to chunk information into meaningful categories. For example, a teacher could say, "Imagine the main character at the beginning, in the middle, and at the end of the story. Imagine what questions you might like to ask her at each particular point in the story." In other content areas, instead of *beginning, middle,* and *end,* the three acts could be *introduction, development,* and *resolution.* Science or social studies students could imagine a solution to pollution, how they might develop their solution, and how it resolves the problem. This "thinking in threes" provides students with a structure that enables them to free up their imagination.

Tina Seelig (2012) described three ways to increase imagination. The first way is to **pay attention to how a question is framed.** The frame directs the imagining of the response. A good way to illustrate this for students is to use humor. For example, in an ocean unit, students were learning that when the sea squirt attaches itself to something and doesn't move on, it will eat its own brain. In response to the teacher's challenge for students to use the content of the lesson to create a joke, one student came up with "Why does the sea squirt eat its own brain? I heard it wants to get smarter." This may not be the funniest joke in the world, but it does demonstrate the student's level of understanding of the content.

Seelig's second suggestion for targeting imaginative thinking is to **connect and combine ideas.** Ideas may be totally fanciful, realistic or not, practical or not. For example, students learn the effects of ultraviolet (UV) rays on skin. As a result of the harmful effects, we now have UV-protected clothing, sunscreen, and chairs with umbrellas attached to them. Students imagine what else we could connect and combine to protect people from the rays and brainstorm a list of ideas.

Seelig also suggested that a way to spark imagination is to **challenge assumptions.** In the classroom, this is best accomplished through problem scenarios where students are given a situation and explore the assumptions that are implied in the scenario itself and those that are present in the solutions. In the ocean study unit example, the teacher gives students a futuristic scenario: "In the year 2030, scientists discover many seagulls have left the ocean environment and moved to live around fresh water lakes and ponds." The students are asked to imagine this scenario, identify why this might be happening, and list possible effects of the situation.

As discussed in the preceding chapters, it is important to make creative thinking transparent for students. When accessing imagination, explicitly describe the process that you are asking students to undertake. Often when we ask students where they get their ideas, we get a blank stare. As you increase the focus on imagination and creativity in your classroom, ask students to start paying attention to where their ideas come from—just having them pay attention to their ideas is a way of practicing imagination and creativity. As the concept of creativity creeps into students' awareness, they will begin to understand creativity as a metacognitive process.

Targeting Imagination with Standards-Based Activities

In addition to new strategies and classroom activities (such as my "grab and go" ideas), teachers seeking to increase their use of imagination in their classrooms will want to tweak the lessons they already use. Figure 3.3 provided some examples of how to connect standards to focus on different creativity skill areas. Figure 4.2 takes these same standards and illustrates how to tweak the lesson to focus on imagination as well as fluency, flexibility, originality, or elaboration. The goal of each lesson is for students to use their imagination when addressing the specific content-area standard.

As you look at the activities in Figure 4.2, think about the nuances of difference among the four types of creativity skill activities. Then, consider what each student needs in order to be successful with these activities. Teachers differentiate imagination creativity lessons because different students need different levels of support at different times. Sometimes when we are working with students to expand their creative thinking skills and exercise their creativity, we need to provide a foundational understanding of the terms we are using. For example, if we want 3rd grade students to be able to imagine assumptions, they need to know what the word *assumptions* means. For the sample Grade 3 fluency lesson in Figure 4.2, this may mean asking students to imagine how the character Caleb might in turn imagine his birth mother. Then, use Pearson's three-act structure to help students chunk out their ideas into three categories: positives, negatives, and assumptions. Model how to identify the assumption in each case by providing students with a sample response to get them started.

Similarly, the 5th grade students reading Carl Sandburg's "Fog" (1916) are expected to know and understand the poem and

FIGURE 4.2

Targeting Imagination Within Creative, Standards-Based Activities

CCSS Key Ideas and Details	**Fluency**	**Flexibility**	**Originality**	**Elaboration**
Grade 3: Ask and answer questions to demonstrate understanding of a text, referring explicitly to the text as the basis for the answers. (RL.3.1) Text: *Sarah, Plain and Tall* (MacLachlan, 1985)	Small groups of students imagine what Caleb assumes about his birth mother. They make a chart listing both positive and negative assumptions. Then, students turn Caleb into a cartoon or comic book character and create a series of frames that include thought bubbles summarizing Caleb's assumptions, also providing text references.	Small groups of students imagine the type of mother Sarah was. They list information in the book that supports their thinking and use their imagination to list information that is missing. They provide references to the text where the changes to the storyline would occur, and discuss how this might affect the overall story arc.	Students individually list or create a chart summarizing what they think, wonder, and imagine about Caleb. Students try to come up with ideas that nobody else will conceive.	Students use a "use your senses" grid to elaborate on the character Sarah. Students imagine how to use the words to generate a paragraph about Sarah. They write the paragraph.

FIGURE 4.2 — (*continued*)

Targeting Imagination Within Creative, Standards-Based Activities

CCSS Key Ideas and Details	Fluency	Flexibility	Originality	Elaboration
Grade 5: Quote accurately from a text when explaining what the text says explicitly and when drawing inferences from the text. (RL.5.1) Text: "Fog" (Sandburg, 1916)	Students imagine and list what else fog moves like other than a cat. Students choose their favorite idea from the list and create a new poem that connects the movements described in the poem with something other than a cat, while maintaining the same inferences from the text.	Students imagine what it would be like to be out in a boat in the ocean in fog. Students maximize or minimize the size of the boat and make changes in the poem to reflect the boat's size.	Students imagine what moves like fog, with the goal of developing an original idea. They write statements that represent their animal/thing without giving away what it is. Other students in the class try to guess what the animal/thing is. Students must support their guesses by referring to examples from the text.	Students imagine what it would be like to be fog. They continue the poem by creating a visual journey, in first person, of where the fog moves next. The visualization they create must include lots of detail and imagery.
Grade 5: Use place value understanding to round decimals to any place. (5.NBT)	Students imagine what a board game looks like that fits on a desk and contains questions that all require rounding decimals. Students list many decimals to round and create their games, with questions relating to the decimals on their lists.	Students create an "agree/disagree/imagine" chart that lists reasons why they agree decimals and place value are important, disagree they are important, and imagine why other people might think decimals and place value are important.	Groups of students imagine and then create an original scavenger hunt for their classmates. They create mathematical clue cards that require players to round decimals or they create clues to find decimals that are rounded.	Students explore the idea of a "guided visualization," and create one that describes rounding decimals. Students need to incorporate a lot of detail in their guided visualizations.

FIGURE 4.2 — (*continued*)

Targeting Imagination Within Creative, Standards-Based Activities

CCSS Key Ideas and Details	Fluency	Flexibility	Originality	Elaboration
High school: Create equations that describe numbers or relationships: Create equations in two or more variables to represent relationships between quantities; graph equations on coordinate axes with labels and scales. (HSA-CED.A.2)	Students imagine many ways to fasten a 3-dimensional *x* or *y* to a 3-dimensional graph and to reuse the variables. Students create the 3-dimensional objects. Students create many cards with one equation with two unknowns on each. Students choose a card from another student and place the 3D variables on the 3D graph.	Students conduct research on a topic of their choice. They create equations with two or more variables to represent their data. They graph their equations to create a presentation (in a format of their choosing) on their research findings without telling other students what their research is about. Others must use their imaginations and think flexibly to guess the topic.	Groups of students imagine how they will perform a math equation and the graphing of the equation; the students use their bodies to represent the variables and the axes. Groups perform an original skit demonstrating the relationship between two quantities and graph them.	Students imagine and then create a multimedia poster that shows how to create equations with two or more variables and graph them. Students include quotes, thought bubbles, and/or music to enhance the effect of the poster.
High school: Cite strong and thorough textual evidence to support analysis of what the text says explicitly as well as inferences drawn from the text, including determining where the text leaves matters uncertain. (RL.12.1) Text: Keats's "Ode on a Grecian Urn": "Beauty is truth, truth beauty,—that is all / Ye know on earth, and all ye need to know."	Students imagine what else the urn could be, by transforming it to many different objects that can tell a story. Students choose which transformation they want to use in their new "Ode on a Grecian Urn."	Students use their imagination to think of many different factors that might have caused Keats to write the poem. Students list their factors and check for flexible thinking. They conduct research to see if they can find evidence of the accuracy or inaccuracy of their assumptions.	Students create an avatar that makes sense contextually (although uniquely) within the parameters of the ode. Students imagine how their presence affects the ode. They rewrite the poem to reflect this new turn of events, retaining the structure and style of the original.	Students imagine the urn speaking its message ("Beauty is truth, truth beauty"). Students elaborate on this message by creating a word cloud. Students present their word clouds to the class; they choose the type of presentation (poster, PowerPoint, multimedia, sound effects, etc.) to enhance their conception.

Note. CCSS = Common Core State Standards (National Governors Association Center for Best Practices, Council of Chief State School Officers, 2010a, 2010b).

its imagery. Because the fluency activity requires them to relate the characteristics of fog to many other things, it also requires them to know what fog is before they let their imaginations run wild.

It may be very difficult for students who live in an area where fog is rare to capture the spirit of the poem. Showing students videos so that they can see how fog rolls in and out will help them grasp the concept. The same idea applies to the flexibility activity; some students have never been in a boat. To enhance imagination, provide visuals and background information when necessary.

When adapting lessons to be more imaginative, it can be helpful to use images as well as words to help students who have trouble with conceptual understanding. Students who have difficulty expressing their ideas in writing can create PowerPoint presentations, posters, and videos to show rather than tell their understanding. This is the idea behind the 12th grade elaboration activity where students make a word cloud (see, e.g., Wordle, www.wordle.net).

Teachers help students recapture their imagination by addressing it as a metacognitive process. Students use their imaginations all the time in math. They imagine finding an answer in their heads. They use mental math to compute answers in their minds. They use their imagination to visualize many shapes, proportions, dimensions, distances, and so on. In the 5th grade math example, students use flexible thinking to determine why they agree and disagree that decimals and place value are important. Then, they use their imagination to think why other people might think decimals are important.

Teachers may need to scaffold lessons when targeting originality and imagination by modeling the process: have the class brainstorm many ideas, then discuss how different their ideas are from one another before identifying which are truly original ideas. (It may be helpful to note for students that the idea they like best may not necessarily be the most original.) Playing a variation on 20 Questions, where students list 10 attributes of an animal or thing without naming it and having other students guess (see "Grab and Go" Idea #24), can also help students exercise their imaginative original thinking. (This idea is illustrated in Figure 4.2 in the Grade 5 example.)

When working with students on elaboration, it is important to stress that students be prepared to defend their ideas by referring to the text or concept. Elaboration must build on not just imagined knowledge but imagined knowledge built from the information presented in the original material. For English language arts, their ideas must make sense contextually; in other content areas, their elaboration needs to fit within the parameters of the content information.

Designing Lessons to Target Creativity and Imagination

The parts of a lesson are the same whether creativity is targeted in the lesson or not. In a lesson accessing imagination, the language the teacher uses, the modeling, the examples that are provided, and the formative and summative assessments address creative thinking about the content. The words the teacher uses helps students to understand that their imaginative thinking will help them to make meaning of the content. The teacher promotes metacognition by asking students to think about their thinking, and clearly identifies the creative aspects of the lesson to focus student attention on those processes.

Figure 4.3 illustrates how to design a lesson to target creative thinking and imagination. In this 5th grade classroom, students are studying Colonial America. In this unit, students learn why people came to America, how the colonies were established, what Colonial life was like, who the famous people were of the times, and the causes and effects of famous events. This particular lesson focuses on the effects of historical changes on daily life.

The teacher has decided that students will use their imaginations combined with facts to compare and contrast causes and effects of influences on daily life in the 1700s, current day, and the year 2050, and share their ideas in a written product: a "back to the future" letter (see "Grab and Go" Idea #21).

In designing her lesson plan to target creative thinking and imagination, the teacher follows a process similar to that illustrated in Figure 3.1. She first identifies the standards—content, topics, subtopics, and concepts—as well as the skills she wants to promote. The teacher also notes the essential question addressed in the unit, the type of assessment she will use to gauge student mastery, and any differentiation she must incorporate to respond to student needs. Next, the teacher decides what she will do to "hook" student interest. In Chapter 1, I discussed how creativity can be promoted in the classroom through creative questioning that sparks student inquiry, the use of unusual images, asking students to connect content to unrelated ideas, and the development of creative products. The teacher in this example uses visuals (i.e., pictures of famous people) as a hook to engage students in the lesson: she asks the students to guess what these people might have in common. Students generate questions using verbs that are posted around the room. The teacher responds to the questions the students pose. Through the course of their questioning, students learn that these people all lived and made discoveries during Colonial times. The teacher then moves into the formal set-up of the lesson and the activity, reviewing the content, thinking process, and product. Note that the teacher highlights for students that she wants them to use their imagination and original thinking in the assignment.

The goal of the lesson is for students to use their imaginations combined with facts to compare and contrast causes and effects of influences on daily life. To help students generate multiple creative ideas, she reads them the following scenario:

FIGURE 4.3

<table>
<tr><th colspan="7">Designing a Lesson: Targeting Creativity and Imagination</th></tr>
<tr><td>Identify Standards, Content, Topics, Subtopics, Skills</td><td colspan="2">CCSS addressed:
• RI.5.1–5.3
• RI.5.7
• W.5.1
• W.5.3
• W.5.4</td><td>Topics:
• Evolution of America
• Life changes
• Characteristics of American colonies</td><td colspan="2">Subtopics:
• Religion
• Economics
• Nationalities
• Climate</td><td>Skills:
• Critical thinking: cause and effect
• Creative thinking: imagination and fluency + originality
• Letter writing</td></tr>
<tr><td>Essential Question</td><td colspan="6">How do events in history influence changes in the daily lives of humans?</td></tr>
<tr><td>Assessment</td><td colspan="6">Formative: rubric</td></tr>
<tr><td>Differentiation</td><td colspan="2">Ability
Reading: different reading levels
Writing: requirements modified</td><td colspan="2">Interest
No differentiation</td><td colspan="2">Cognitive style
No differentiation</td></tr>
<tr><td>"Hook" Student Interest</td><td colspan="6">Teacher shows students images of Ben Franklin, Eli Whitney, Joseph Priestly, and Anders Celsius: Let's use our imaginations. What do you think these people might have in common?
Students ask questions about the individuals; discussion leads to information that all of them made amazing discoveries in the 1770s (Franklin: bifocals, daylight saving time; Whitney: cotton gin; etc.).</td></tr>
<tr><td>Lesson Set-Up</td><td colspan="2">Teacher reviews/extends content:
• Reminds students of Internet sites they have explored for information about the colonies.
• Students brainstorm a list of information that they learned through their web searches.</td><td colspan="2">Teacher reviews the thinking process:
The teacher reminds students of a previous lesson where they used their imagination to help them think originally.</td><td colspan="2">Teacher reviews the product form: The teacher presents the "back to the future" letter product. She reminds students that imagined scenarios are based on facts and are logical extensions of real ideas. Students must make sure the letter includes real and imagined content and is written in a unique way.</td></tr>
</table>

FIGURE 4.3 — (*continued*)

Designing a Lesson: Targeting Creativity and Imagination		
The Activity	Introduction: The teacher tells students they will use their imaginations combined with facts to compare and contrast causes and effects of influences on daily life in the 1700s, 2014, and 2050s, and share their ideas in a "back to the future" letter.	Procedures: Students write or draw their initial ideas, to use when they write their letters. Teacher notes that • Students can use any resources for background information to put in their letter. A variety of reader-level resources are available. • Students may help each other. • The assignment focuses on original thinking; the ideas they present as well as the way they present them will be assessed in terms of originality. • The teacher makes adjustments in the writing requirement for some students. Teacher discusses the rubric for the assignment with students and provides the students with a timetable for completion of their product. Students complete the rubric and share responses with the whole class. The teacher provides each student feedback by completing the rubric.
Assessment	Students use the rubric to **self-assess** at the draft stage. The teacher assesses the final draft using the rubric and provides students with written feedback to supplement scoring on the rubric.	

> Imagine you are a time traveler about to travel to America in the 1770s. Of the New England, Middle, and Southern colonies, you decide to go to the same area where you live now. What do you see? Use your imagination to describe it. Craft a letter to take with you when you time travel describing what you know about the region during their time, your time, and what you imagine it will be like in the future. Make sure to write this letter in a way that makes them believe you are from a different time.

After presenting the scenario, the students make some notes about their ideas. The teacher gives them choices in how they want to do this: they can write a list, draw some images, or complete a graphic organizer. The teacher also differentiates instruction by providing a graphic organizer template to any student who would like to use one. For the assignment, students have a choice as to which and how many resources they use. The resources available to them reflect different reading levels.

The rubric for the assignment (Figure 4.4) provides students with clear expectations for their product and also serves as a self-assessment tool. In addition to providing an overview of the content-related requirements, the rubric specifically describes the need for students to use creative thinking (i.e., originality) and their imagination to come up with reasonable, logical ideas that could have influenced or affected situations in the past, the present, and the future. As noted above, the assignment incorporates controlled student choice; they can express themselves uniquely in the writing style that they choose. The standard targets clear and coherent writing; this is also incorporated into the assignment. Because the assignment product is considered a final draft, students need to avoid grammatical and spelling errors. The written product requirements can be differentiated for students who have difficulty expressing their ideas in writing, and their rubric would be slightly modified.

FIGURE 4.4

Sample Rubric for Lesson Targeting Creativity and Imagination

Product Element	Not So Hot	Okay	Very Good	Great
Colonial times: Daily life Political involvement Religious freedom Wealth opportunities	Few facts Little or no evidence of research Facts only Little detail	Some facts Some evidence of research Facts with few additional imagined details	Many facts Evidence of research Facts combined with some details; one or two logical, imagined ideas; at least one original idea	Many facts Evidence of extensive research Facts combined with many original, logical imagined ideas that enhance the scenario Many details that add emotion and tone to the content information
Current day: Daily life Political involvement Religious freedom Wealth opportunities	Few facts Little or no evidence of research Facts only Little detail	Some facts Some evidence of research Facts with few additional imagined details	Many facts Evidence of research	Many facts Evidence of extensive research Facts combined with many original, logical imagined ideas that enhance the scenario Many details that add emotion and tone to the content information

FIGURE 4.4 — (*continued*)

Sample Rubric for Lesson Targeting Creativity and Imagination

Product Element	Not So Hot	Okay	Very Good	Great
Future: Daily life Political involvement Religious freedom Wealth opportunities	Few facts Little or no evidence of research Facts only Little detail	Some facts Some evidence of research Facts with few additional imagined details	Many facts Evidence of research Facts combined with some details; one or two logical, imagined ideas; at least one original idea	Many facts Evidence of extensive research Facts combined with many original, logical imagined ideas that enhance the scenario Many details that add emotion and tone to the content information
Compare and contrast	Makes few, obvious, or illogical points	Makes some points, but many are obvious	Makes many points, some of which are inferential	Makes many original points
"Back to the future" letter	Tone or expression is confusing Format or writing style is confusing Writing is not coherent Spelling and grammar mistakes	Tone or expression is confusing in one or two places Format or writing style is basic Writing is mostly coherent No spelling or grammar mistakes	Correct use of tone and expression Original use of format or writing style Clear, coherent writing No spelling or grammar mistakes	Original use of tone and expression Original use of format or writing style Clear, coherent writing No spelling or grammar mistakes

The teacher works with students in small groups as needed, and has developed an interactive blog for the assignment that students and parents can access; if students have questions while working at home on the assignment, they can post their questions and get help.

This sample lesson requires students to do both critical and creative thinking. Accessing creative thinking helps students think more critically about content (Treffinger, Schoonover, & Selby, 2013). A constant thread of creative thinking runs throughout this lesson: students use their imagination when they listen to the guided visualization, when they compare and contrast, and in their choice of product form. This is a clear example of how creativity is connected to critical thinking and not just fun, carefree thinking; creative thinking about content drives depth of understanding and fosters long-term learning.

Encouraging Imaginative Thinking

Teachers foster imagination by sharing with students their own imaginative thinking. For example, tell students when a story did not end the way you imagined it would, or how a movie was not what you imagined when you read the book.

Teachers also can encourage imagination by helping students understand how imagination allows us to play with possibilities and make connections. It allows us to form images and concepts while providing meaning to experiences. To encourage students' imagination to grow, teachers must believe imagination plays a role in students' thinking, believe students can use imaginative thinking as a platform to construct deep meaning in a variety of content areas, and, finally, believe that imagination has a role to play in education.

The 17 "grab and go" ideas included at the end of this chapter are strategies that teachers can use to help students access imaginative thinking in order to promote learning. These strategies, like those in the preceding chapters, target four areas of creativity: fluency, flexibility, originality, and elaboration—except this time, they also promote imaginative thinking. The strategies are primarily from Creativity Roads 1 and 2.

Many of the strategies are flexible (i.e., can be altered to target a different area of creativity), and some can be used to target a combination of creativity areas. In this case, when presenting the activity to students, be sure to specify the type of thinking or result you are seeking (e.g., by naming and including a rubric). For example, when targeting flexibility and originality, students should know the goal is for them to generate different ideas—of which one is "one of a kind."

Reflecting on and Extending Chapter Information

1. Defend or refute: imagination is critical to creative thinking.
2. In an education setting, why is it important for students to understand that imagination is not just for young children?
3. How can you integrate imaginative thinking into your content?
4. People often associate imaginative thinking with visualization. What would you say to students who, after visualization, say they do not "see" anything?
5. Why is it important to address imaginative thinking across content areas and grade levels?

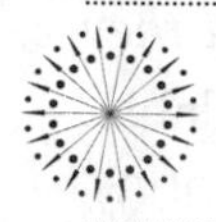

"Grab and Go" Idea #15

Imagination Word Prompts

As with "Grab and Go" Idea #1, when targeting fluency along with imagination, have students generate lists of many alternatives, focusing on a specific topic, idea, or concept. When targeting flexibility, use phrases that denote differences. This strategy is found on Creativity Road 1. Using the following words and terms can also spark students' imagination:

- Imagine
- Just suppose
- What if
- What would
- Adjust
- Transform
- Symbolize
- Visualize

"Grab and Go" Idea #16

KWW Chart

Wonder is a powerful word to use with students, and it is a great way to access imagination. Using the word *wonder* stimulates the imagination and requires students to extend their thinking about what they know and understand. The thought-provoking question "What do you wonder about...?" is applicable to any content area.

Most teachers are familiar with KWL charts (Ogle, 1986), which help students organize what they know, what they want to know, and, later, what they learned. The typical KWL chart can be adapted to incorporate imaginative thinking; students can list what they know, what they want to know, and *what they wonder about*. (The KWW chart can also be recast as a foldable, three-dimensional interactive graphic organizer; see Zike, 2000). Teachers can ask all three questions as part of a preassessment or they can isolate the imagination element by asking students to answer the "wonder" question as a formative assessment, partway through a unit, or as part of a summative assessment to see what students still wonder about at the end of a unit. The KWW chart can be used to target both content information and fluency, by encouraging students to fill in more than one response in each column. When a student only fills in one response, the student is not doing much thinking, just responding with the first thing that comes to mind.

The KWW chart can also be adapted further, for use at the end of a lesson or unit, as a tool for students to record what the content information makes them think about, wonder about, and imagine (TWI). This is a strategy that is found on Creativity Road 2. These types of questions require students to use the information and imagine beyond the known.

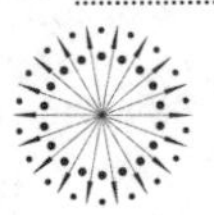

"Grab and Go" Idea #17

Plus, Minus, Assumptions

This strategy, also found on Creativity Road 2, is designed to help students identify and evaluate assumptions; it supports students in applying content information while also using creative thinking skills to elaborate on information in the text. For this activity, students think of many positive and negative ideas about the content, and then generate a list of many possible assumptions.

For example, in a Colonial America 5th grade unit, students are learning about the Boston Massacre. Students learn about the propaganda that was used to enrage the colonists against the British (e.g., Paul Revere engraving). After reading information from different websites, students think about the plusses, minuses, and assumptions that are reflected by a particular point of view. Their imagined assumptions must be logical, possible assumptions that could have been made by either faction (colonist or British); students must be able to provide evidence supporting their ideas. Students pair up with other students to share their responses.

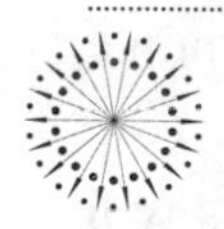

"Grab and Go" Idea #18

Information / Missing Information

This Creativity Road 2 strategy reminds students to question information rather than assume information is complete. Students already do this in their mathematics classes, when they are given a math problem that they cannot solve because there is not enough information. Information / Missing Information takes this idea one step further by asking students to imagine and then list many possible pieces of missing information and reasons why the different pieces of information might be missing.

For example, in literacy, teachers ask students to list and defend what we know and do not know about a character or situation in a story. What do we know and not know about the author of the story and why? In science, in a 7th grade genetics unit, students list and defend what they know and do not know about genetic diversity. In a high school class, students are studying global and regional interdependence. After reading the chapter in their textbook, the teacher asks students to list information about the role of the United Nations secretary-general when faced with a humanitarian crisis and imagine and list information or questions that the textbook did not address and possible reasons why the author chose not to address these issues.

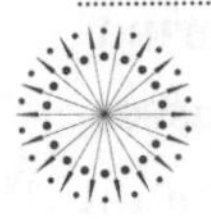

"Grab and Go" Idea #19

Transformation

Transformation is a visual strategy that requires the student to transform an image or idea into something else. It is often used to enhance students' memory of content information and aid recall.

For example, an elementary teacher finds that her early learners often confuse a rhombus and a trapezoid. She gives half of the students a rhombus and half of the students a trapezoid, and asks them to imagine what the shape could be. Students change their shape into something else by adding lines, circles, and so on. After they use their shape a few times or so, most students will remember the name of their shape. Students partner with someone who has the other shape to share responses.

This strategy can be used when discussing a character, explorer, mathematician, or scientist; students are asked to draw or visualize the person in eight different situations. Teachers also can guide a class to take a symbol representing a concept (e.g., the rainforest, ecology, the U.S. Constitution), and then transform it into something else. Students can even take a seminal year such as 1776 and transform the numbers into a variety of images. The point of the lesson is not the actual transformations that occur, but that students use the strategy to drive content information into long-term memory. As such, the creative emphasis is not on Creativity Road 4, the product; it is on Creativity Road 2, the process.

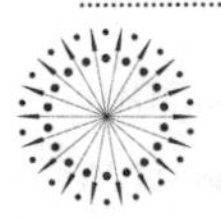

"Grab and Go" Idea #20

Cues, Context, and Point of View

Interpretation is a powerful strategy that can be used in a variety of content areas. This strategy facilitates students' practice of flexible thinking and shows them how cues, context, and point of view influence interpretation. Interpretation is also based upon a context that comprises time, place, and situation. The context can remain the same regardless of the changes in visual cue and point of view. The strategy itself uses a visual cue to introduce students to interpretation and is found on Creativity Road 2.

For example, in a high school social studies unit, the teacher shows students an image of a child laborer in the 1940s and asks them to imagine what they think the child's life is like. Students list their ideas based upon what they see and on what they know about the situation at the time (i.e., content knowledge). The teacher changes the picture to an adult and asks students to do the same thing. Some students may think the picture is the parent of the child, whereas others think the picture is the owner of a factory. Discussing the various and different interpretations opens the door to a discussion about life in the 1940s. Asking students to provide information from their content knowledge to back up their interpretations helps solidify their understanding.

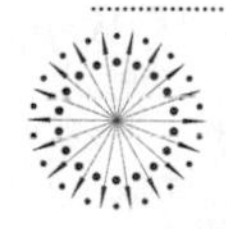

"Grab and Go" Idea #21

"Back to the Future" Letter

This strategy, which emphasizes Creativity Roads 2 and 4, promotes flexible thinking by having students imagine different scenarios. For the exercise, students pretend they can time travel. First, they "find" a letter that was written in the past; the letter can be teacher-generated, or could be the result of collaborative class discussion. Students then write individual responses about what was, what is now, and what they think will be.

For example, in their study of the Industrial Revolution, students in one class "found" a letter that described why people migrated from farms to mill life in the cities. The students wrote back a letter about the situation during the Industrial Revolution, their current time, and what they projected future migration would be in 25 years. In a Greek mythology unit, students "received" a letter from Theseus describing how heroic behavior influences others. The students imagined the content of the letter, then commented on it, and discussed the influence of heroic behavior in their own time and the impact future heroic behavior might have.

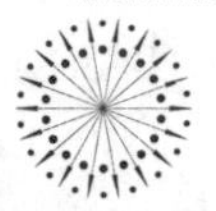

"Grab and Go" Idea #22

Three Wishes

Three Wishes encourages students to imagine and think flexibly about the content they are learning. This Creativity Road 2 strategy requires students to generate multiple different ideas surrounding a single topic.

For example, at the elementary level, a teacher tells students that they are magical and have the power to grant wishes. They meet a character in the story the class is reading. Asked to imagine what the character might ask for, they list many different wishes that make sense in the context of the story.

At the secondary level, teachers can use the same strategy but frame the question differently. For example, as part of a coming-of-age literature unit, the teacher has students paraphrase passages that identify or suggest physical and personality characteristics. Given this information, students imagine three wishes the character might desire. They list the wishes and back them up with evidence from the paraphrased passages.

Another secondary example is from a physics class. After the class discusses the major obstacles in having a new theory accepted, the teacher asks students to imagine they have created a new theory and that they are granted three wishes. What are their wishes, and why? Again, the wishes must make sense within the parameters of the unit's content, and students need to provide the reasoning behind their ideas.

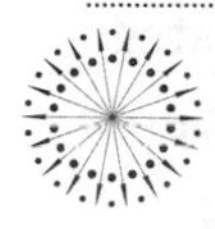

"Grab and Go" Idea #23

Voice Changes

This strategy helps students think flexibly about the content, enhances their ability to communicate effectively, and can help them master certain facts or processes they are learning. It directs their attention, too, to what they are hearing (similar to the use of sound effects in "Grab and Go" Idea #4). How the strategy is used varies by content. The students use their imagination to determine the impact of their voice change on the audience.

For example, in a persuasive writing unit, students share their writing with others and use voice changes to dramatize the dialogue representing different points of view. The teacher might ask students to change their tone, pitch, or volume when they read a major point, when they read a supporting detail, or when they change topics. In this case, students use their voice flexibly in order to facilitate the audience's understanding of the content.

This strategy supports student mastery of content knowledge. If students are having difficulty remembering to reverse the second fraction before dividing fractions, for example, the strategy can be used when thinking out loud about how to solve the math problem. When describing the process, the student speaks more loudly when discussing the reverse of the second fraction than during the rest of the explanation. This ensures that other students pay particular attention to this part of the explanation. The strategy can be further adapted by having other students figure out precisely what concept, process, or idea the voice change is emphasizing. Both Creativity Roads 2 and 4 are applied in this strategy.

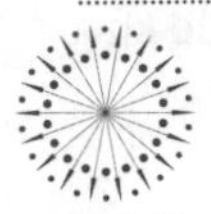

"Grab and Go" Idea #24

10 Statements

Similar to the game 20 Questions, this Creativity Road 2 strategy is geared toward developing students' original thinking. Students choose an image or quotation, place it on one side of a card or into a PowerPoint document, and share it with the rest of the class. On the back of the card or on the second slide the student creates an original true statement that they think nobody else can guess. This strategy pushes students to extract and use information they think nobody else will think of—the information, however, must be significant and relevant to the content.

This strategy really encourages students to think beyond the obvious content information, and to use their imagination to anticipate what their fellow classmates will say. It is also effective as a group review before a test or at the end of a unit.

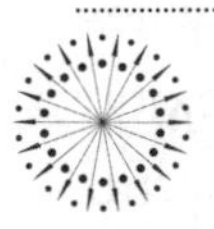

"Grab and Go" Idea #25

Advertising Trailers

Like a movie trailer, an advertising trailer sets the stage to engage learners by hooking their interest. The Advertising Trailer strategy requires students to summarize content information creatively, imagine, and then design an original trailer—and communicate with an audience. This strategy is a great example of Creativity Roads 2 and 4. This activity also requires students to use powerful verbs and images in order to grab other students' attention. They might start out with an "I wonder…" statement or a "Did you ever consider…?" statement. They might start out with a bold statement such as "Relationships are not always what they appear." The end of the advertising trailer should include a book, an Internet article, or another print source for more information;

this also ensures that students use reliable sources for their information. Students can make their trailer using multimedia or "old style" trailers with pen and pencil. The incorporation of visuals adds another layer both to enhancing creative thinking and imagining and to mastery of content.

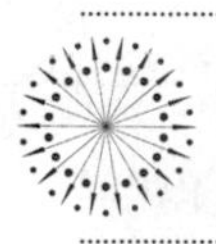

"Grab and Go" Idea #26

Avatars

An avatar is a computer-generated character that lives in a virtual world. This strategy can be used whether students have computer access or not, to encourage creative thinking by accessing students' imaginations and emotions. This activity requires students to create themselves as a character and place themselves in the content. They do not actually access a virtual world on the computer; they imagine it. As such, it is a Creative Road 2 strategy. They should describe what they see, hear, and feel as a result of being in this new world.

For example, in an elementary math unit, the teacher asked students to create an avatar for themselves and enter the world of polygons. In this world, they meet up with six or more different types of polygons. What do they see? How do they feel? Are there any conflicts? Are there any polygon issues? Students need to understand that even though this mathematical world is fantastical, their responses must still make sense. Another example of an avatar adventure is to go inside Earth's crust to explore volcanoes. What is happening? What do you do? Who else is there? What evidence do you find that supports the theory of plate tectonics?

In introducing the avatar concept and purpose of the exercise, teachers can use video games as an example: these are not real worlds, but we sometimes feel like they are. The appeal of this activity to students sparks imagination. They can give themselves powers, strengths, and abilities beyond what is human. However, the challenge is to blend the fantastic with the real. There must be reason behind their cause-and-effect decisions. Their imaginary travels must demonstrate real content information.

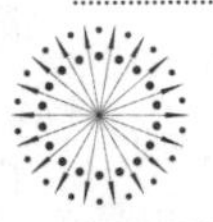

"Grab and Go" Idea #27

Scavenger Hunt

Most students love the idea of a scavenger hunt. This is a great activity to combine both imagination and technology, as the "scavenger hunt" is on the Internet and is a hunt for information, much like a webquest (see http://webquest.org/). The point of the strategy is for students to imagine how the scavenger hunt will be laid out and create it—and for the teacher to ensure that deep content learning is happening.

The activity requires students to use their imagination to come up with original ideas (Creativity Road 2) of things to "hunt" for, to create clues, and to find websites. The most common iteration of this strategy has students pose a question and other students find answers. The questioning student can create clues to lead students to websites where they will collect information that helps them discover the answer. Because a good scavenger hunt takes time to create (Creativity Road 4), this activity makes a good homework assignment.

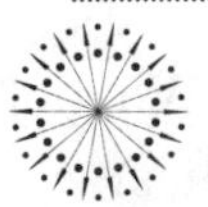

"Grab and Go" Idea #28

Guided Visualization

A guided visualization is where the student listens to an audio piece and imagines what is going on. This activity can be done a couple of different of ways, both of which require students to elaborate on content. This activity is a Creative Road 2 strategy and also can be a Creative Road 4 strategy, depending upon the product in the lesson.

To introduce the activity, the teacher first conducts a guided visualization. For example, in a medieval unit, the teacher has students close their eyes and imagine a feast celebrating a marriage:

> The feast takes place in a huge hall with ceilings so high you can barely see the ceiling. The colors are bright and vivid on the paintings, on the patterns on the carpets, and on the ladies' dresses. The noise surrounds you as you focus on a conversation nearby. The serfs are bringing in the food, and the smell is overwhelming. Your mouth is watering. You notice crumbs are falling everywhere.

The teacher can either conclude with "You are a mouse. Describe your experience," and have students generate a written project, or the guided visualization can be followed by an extensive class discussion about the details students added with their imaginations during the visualization. This in turn could be followed with students creating their own guided visualizations, building on the same premise. In both cases, students need to exercise their creative thinking skills and imagination to provide rich and vivid detail in their written product.

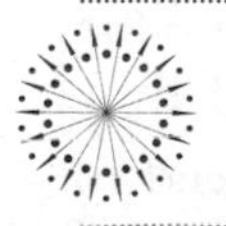

"Grab and Go" Idea #29

Graphic Summaries

Graphic summaries encourage students to use their imagination and their elaboration skills. The graphic summary allows students to think originally about content and elaborate on what they read through the use of vivid language and creative visuals. This emphasizes Creative Roads 2 and 4. At least some of the graphics should be symbolic and not literal; students' writing should incorporate appropriate content language and concepts. The incorporation of graphics allows students to personalize their writing by creating mood, tone, and nuance.

For example, in a 5th grade historical fiction unit, students read one of two books—one a fictionalized retelling of the Donner Party expedition, and one a "diary" of child on the Oregon Trail—and then create a graphic summary of a day in the life of the main character. A high school teacher I know uses graphic summaries to help students understand the relevance of naturally occurring mathematical patterns. His students create graphic summaries interpreting functions in science whose patterns are used for prediction (e.g., growth and decay functions, exponential functions in a scientific/futuristic endeavor). Graphic summaries can be adapted for all content areas and grade levels; the rubric provides guidance to students on length, number of graphics to include, and other elements the teacher will use to assess both content mastery and creative thinking.

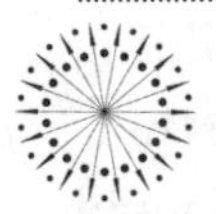

"Grab and Go" Idea #30

Visualize-Draw-Write

The Visualize-Draw-Write strategy (Pearson, 1997) makes much more sense than having students write something and *then* draw a picture. When they write first, students often complain they have nothing to write about or they cannot get started. If they draw first, they have something to write about. All they need to do is look at their drawing and they can get started writing about it. The "drawing" can be a basic representation of the information (a literal drawing), a graphic organizer, or computer generated, depending on content and grade level. The strategy focuses on Creativity Road 2.

In an elementary grade weather unit, the teacher described a changing front: "The clouds changed from white, puffy—*cumulus*—clouds to dark, tall clouds. The wind began to die. It was perfectly still. Suddenly, the wind picked up and started to blow, hard." At this point, she asked students to visualize what would happen next. They drew pictures of what they visualized, then used elaborative language to describe everything that was in their pictures or associated with the images in their pictures.

"Grab and Go" Idea #31

GE (Generate and Elaborate)

The GE strategy uses original and elaborative thinking and imagination to reinforce content knowledge and expand vocabulary. Students imagine the concept, then generate a list of words associated with the concept. They choose one of the words from their list on which to elaborate. This is considered a Creativity Road 2 strategy.

For example, in a social studies unit, students imagine what they know about discrimination and list words associated with it. They choose the most powerful word from their list. They describe their personal meaning of the chosen word. They look up the word in a dictionary to see if the dictionary definition adds a different aspect to the meaning.

Teachers can extend this strategy by having students create a word cloud (see, e.g., www.wordle.net). Word clouds can be altered with different fonts, colors, and layouts, or words can be clustered together to create different shapes. The use of color can create dramatic effects. After students create their word cloud, they describe how the terms relate to the overall concept.

Creativity and Innovation

Cultivating Innovative Ideas and Action

Innovative ideas come from a slow hunch, sudden insight, or pure chance (Johnson, 2010). Sometimes one idea mingles with another idea to form a hunch, and it turns into something new. Innovation can come from collaborating with others (Sawyer, 2006a; Wagner, 2012) or from having the time to explore one's thoughts alone. Inspiration can come from everyday sources, passions and interests, or the unconscious mind. Many innovations are the result of solving problems, making improvements, and real-life investigation; others combine existing innovations. Wagner (2012) interviewed innovators and found a commonality: they all visualized their ideas and mentally figured out what they needed to do to achieve their goals.

According to Govindarajan (2010), innovation prevents creativity from growing stale. Although creative thinkers produce worthwhile ideas, some believe they will not be useful to society if they cannot take action on their ideas. Our creativity enables us to come up with great ideas; our innovation enables us to execute them. Robinson described it thus: "Innovation is applied creativity" (2011, Chapter 6).

Imagination, creativity, and innovation are interrelated. Imagination sparks innovation. Creativity helps us to produce ideas. Innovation allows us to both generate and apply creative ideas in a given context. According to Robinson, "Innovation is the process of putting original ideas into practice" (2011, Chapter 9).

Promoting Innovation in the Creative Classroom

Innovation in the classroom often occurs as part of a problem-based unit. Students identify problems or challenges based on a given scenario, conduct investigations, and develop an innovative solution. This is the nature of innovation: it serves a purpose, responds to an identified need, and provides a solution. To support students' practice in this area of creativity, ask guiding questions such as the following:

- What is the need? What is the problem or challenge in this situation?
- What is different? Is your innovation worth pursuing? How is your work or idea different from other work or ideas that have been tried or done before?
- What is the solution? How and why do you think your idea is the solution to a problem?
- What is problematic? What problems might surface as a result of your innovation and how will you address them?

Another way to support students' understanding of innovation is to specifically identify the steps in the innovative process. For example, a high school physics teacher introduced the innovative process by showing students the procedural process in Figure 5.1 (Creativity Road 3). The students practiced using the process after watching the movie *The Social Network* (Fincher & Sorkin, 2010). The movie describes how Mark Zuckerberg created Facebook, an innovative idea using technology. Students paid special attention to the way Zuckerberg moved his innovative idea from a thought to a valuable product. After students viewed the movie, they used the statements in Figure 5.1 to analyze the process and procedures Zuckerberg used to create Facebook. Sample lessons such as this one help drive understanding about the innovative process. The class discussion focused on Zuckerberg's actions and the element of risk: was he being financially reckless, and, if so, when? This led to the question "Why not stop?" The resulting message that the students took away is this: "Think big."

To help students understand what it takes for a creative idea to become something real, teachers model the innovative process. The more students talk about innovation, analyze others' innovations, and discuss the process, the more comfortable they will be actually using the process to engage in innovation.

Innovation begins with inquiry and ends in action. Students need to be able to generate their own questions or ideas to direct their search for answers and solutions. Students who are adept at creative brainstorming and questioning—that is, those who are fluent in their ability to think of possibilities and generate meaningful questions in their pursuit of knowledge—are able to think of many varied questions to drive inquiry. Students who do not have fluent and flexible creative thinking skills often want to jump right in to innovate without doing the legwork. Figure 5.1's stages can be used to delineate a process and provide a structure that helps students think logically and deeply when analyzing the innovations of others developing their own. Figure 5.1 shows how the teacher used some of the elements of each stage, but not all. Teachers should use whatever elements apply to the lesson. As with other areas of creativity, some students may need additional structure and scaffolding, particularly as regards self-regulation and organizational skills, as they embark on this endeavor.

FIGURE 5.1

The Innovative Process

Stage	Example	Student Response
Brainstorm • Sources of inspiration • Needs based on problems/situations	According to the movie *The Social Network* (2010), where did the idea for Facebook come from?	Mark's idea was based on the other men's social media creation, Harvard FaceMash.
Evaluate • Ideas • Sources of inspiration • Needs based on problems/situations	1. Why did Mark decide to move forward with Facebook? 2. Why did he decide to expand his idea beyond the university community?	1. He wanted to impress the girl. 2. He was driven by a broken heart. The woman wasn't aware of Facebook, so he decided to make its presence bigger.
Identify steps to produce the innovation	What were the steps Mark took to move Facebook from an idea to a huge, successful web presence?	1. He created the website. 2. He moved to California. 3. He made the website global.
Identify the enablers and disablers • People • Situations • Resources	Who enabled Mark's success?	His friend Sean Parker.
	Who presented challenges to Mark's Facebook effort?	The men who created the social media site at Harvard.
Reflect • Endpoint • Degree of effectiveness	How did Mark know when he completed his innovation?	The woman noticed him when Facebook became popular. But his innovation doesn't really have an end-point because Facebook is still expanding and changing.

Teachers in the creative classroom can encourage innovation in several other ways:

- *Give students physical space to innovate.* Create a "think tank" area in the classroom where students can either go individually or gather to explore and exchange ideas.
- *Make innovation intentional.* Frame the goal so that the desired outcome is absolutely clear. Incorporating innovation

into students' daily lives—for example, asking them to identify innovative solutions to the problem of a noisy classroom—makes the process of innovation concrete and shows students its real-life application.

- *Give students time to ponder.* Innovative ideas need time to surface. Major companies that we think of as innovative (e.g., Google, 3M) incorporate "free time" within the workday; this time off allows "employees to explore and the freedom to be creative, which can improve morale and increase work output" (Baldwin, 2012, p. 1). Consider the intentional use of unstructured time; unless there is an immediate need to solve a problem, give students time to think.
- *Let students decide what and how to measure success.* For some students, the challenge is working with an idea that causes the greatest positive impact rather than an idea that they like best. Engage students in determining what is measurable and what results are meaningful. How will they determine to what degree their results are effective?
- *Recognize students for their effort as well as their success.* Continuous reinforcement of effort can help keep students engaged, and will help build students' innovative skills. Recognition, however, must be specific in order to be effective. Smiley faces on a sticky note are only effective if students know what they did to make the teacher smile.

There is a school of thought that believes creativity is social; Sawyer (2006a) noted that "the most important creative insights typically emerge from collaborative teams and creative circles" (p. 42). If we translate this information to a school setting, then teachers should organize collaborative teams of students to tap into the innovation process throughout a project cycle.

It may be effective to teach students to work together and use an improvisational approach (Sawyer, 2006b), spinning off of each other's ideas, with each student inspiring the others to think of new or improved ideas. "Disciplined improvisation leads to deeper understanding than rote learning" (Bransford, Brown, & Cocking, 2000, as cited in Sawyer, 2006a, p. 44). Facilitating collaboration among students means guiding students so that they collaboratively, socially derive meaning from content.

For students to be able to work together effectively and take the leaps of faith required for innovative thinking, they need to be in an environment that is accepting of creativity and risk taking. Students need to feel that it is okay to make mistakes, and that mistakes are necessary on the road to innovation. As with other creative thinking skills, teachers can help students become metacognitively aware of the innovative process. Establishing meaningful definitions and creating shared language surrounding innovation will help students understand the process as well as the importance of innovation and innovative thinking. The shared language promotes innovative thinking by using language that innovators use.

Attending to Executive Function Skills

Executive function skills are key to students' building the "cognitive capacity necessary for school success" (Molfese et al., 2010, as cited in Jensen, 2013, p. 58). To successfully engage in innovation, students need day-to-day executive function skills such as self-control, processing, attention, and memory capacity and sequencing.

When students have issues with **self-control,** they want to jump to a right/wrong conclusion, often one that seems familiar. Innovation is a process, however, that requires self-control with and between the stages in the innovative process. It may help students to follow a step-by-step process, such as in Figure 5.1, to help them stay on task and resist impulsivity.

Another executive function skill area that can present a challenge to students is maintaining **attention and focus.** When we become frustrated by students' lack of attention, we must remember that students usually *are* focused; they just are not focused on what we want them to be. Teachers can boost students' attention and focus by asking them to make a prediction. The process of prediction engages the brain; as Snyder (2013) described, "If the prediction is correct, dopamine reinforces the effort to try again. When it's wrong, the brain wants to try again to get that mental rush" (p. 1). So including prediction in an exercise helps students stay focused—they will want to find out if they are right.

DiSalvo (2011, Chapter 4) observed that "most of us are mentally elsewhere between 30 and 50 percent of our waking hours," and surmised that spacing out serves an important adaptive function: during this time our brains are digesting data. He also added, "Research points to a strong link between mind wandering and creativity" (Chapter 4). This is a benefit to creative thinking (if, that is, students can control their daydreaming). Teachers should not assume that students are not paying attention, listening, or processing information when they daydream. The challenge, though, is determining whether the student spacing out is thinking of nothing, thinking of something other than what the class is discussing, or reflecting longer on whatever the class is discussing. Rather than assume that the daydreaming is a focus and attention problem, teachers should simply ask students what they are thinking about.

Executive function affects **working memory**, which is "a greater predictor of academic success... than IQ" (Alloway & Alloway, 2010, as cited in Jensen, 2013, p. 67). It is nearly impossible for students to be creative about the content if they do not know or cannot remember content. Some techniques and strategies that can help students remember include creative activities, avoiding informational overload, helping students categorize information, utilizing graphic organizers, providing multisensory stimulation, and designing experiential, real-life learning lessons.

One skill that plays an important role in the innovative process is the ability to follow steps in a process. In order to sequence the innovative task, students must be able to **prioritize and organize** information. They need to know what to do when, and in what order. This skill is teachable when the teacher guides and coaches students by using strategies such as

- a graphic organizer that helps students know when to do what, and what is needed at each step;
- modeling the process to accomplish the task;
- reducing the number of steps for accomplishing the task; and
- having students practice the prioritize-and-organize process by arranging the tasks in order.

Utilizing Strategies to Encourage Innovative Thinking

When introducing students to the concept of innovation, teachers can hook students' interest by discussing the U.S. Patent Office and its role in recognizing true innovation. A brief discussion about the Patent Office can help students understand that some ideas fail, or simply are not innovative enough. Many innovations, however, are successful and do end up as products or ideas that make a difference (about 60% of ideas submitted for patent approval are approved). Introducing the idea of the formal patent approval process reinforces student understanding of innovation as a response to a need or problem. This approach can be used in different content areas to springboard students' exploration of the innovative process:

- Students studying World War II look at innovations that received patents during that time. Which ones had to do with a response to the needs of the war? Why was innovation important during that timeframe?

- In a unit focusing on water conservation, students explore the history of bathtubs and showers along with attendant water consumption data. They identify innovative ways that bathing has improved over time and determine whether patents were issued for these innovations.
- Students studying fossil fuels work in collaborative groups to identify a specific problem that exists and come up with an innovation to address the problem. They research whether their innovation already exists, and if so, if there is a patent for the innovation.

After students explore the relationship between innovation and patents, they are ready to apply the innovation process in Figure 5.1 to the content they are studying. Figure 5.2 provides examples of innovation activities across content areas.

FIGURE 5.2

Innovation Activities Across Content Areas

Literacy	Math	Science	Social Studies
• Create an innovation that would improve a character's life. • Create an innovative way to improve communication between two characters. • Develop an innovative way to solve the problem in the story. • Suggest an innovative way for the main character to take a risk.	• Determine an innovative way to remember math facts. • Design an innovative system of measurement. • Create an innovative way to demonstrate parallel operations using scale and manipulatives. • Determine an innovative way to demonstrate place value.	• Identify an innovative way to reduce pollution. • Develop an innovative way to continue space exploration. • Determine an innovative solution to compensate for the loss of a sense. • Create an innovative space object using at least two characteristics.	• Create an innovative solution to a problem in our community. • Describe an innovative solution to the concept of scarcity. • Create an innovative way to celebrate a national holiday. • Develop an innovative form of transportation that will be beneficial to society.

Innovation in the creative classroom can take many forms. For example, a 5th grade teacher presenting a unit on the Westward Movement asks students to come up with an innovative way to improve a Conestoga wagon and actually make their new and improved wagon. This assignment requires students to research how the wagons were used, determine what the needs were at that time, and respond to a need. Groups of students use the innovative process to come up with the innovation and move it forward to something they can actually create. They work together to apply math and the scientific principles of movement and mechanisms to create their modified wagon. If time does not permit, students do not have to actually physically create an innovation; simply analyzing their idea for an innovation using the steps in Figure 5.1 contributes to their understanding of this aspect of creativity.

This process of innovation can be explicitly taught:

1. *Brainstorm* possible needs or problems and ways to respond.
2. *Evaluate* ideas to decide which idea is most worth pursuing.
3. *Identify steps* in the process to produce the modification or improvement.
4. *Identify enablers and disablers* of the idea.
5. *Reflect on the results* of the innovation in order to determine if it is complete or needs to be modified.

Targeting Innovation Within Creative, Standards-Based Activities

As with other areas of creative thinking, innovation can help students gain a deeper understanding of content. To be able to come up with an innovative solution to a problem, students must know and understand the problem described in the text and the topic or concept of the problem. This knowledge is reinforced when the teacher requires students to reference where the text indicates a need, to cite sources identifying a challenge or problem, or to describe the principle underlying a proposed solution. The process of innovation is strengthened for students if the assignment also requires them to explain their thinking throughout.

Figure 5.3 revisits the academic content standards I presented in previous chapters. This time, we are looking at connecting the standard with an activity that targets students' skills in innovation.

In order for any lesson targeting innovation to be successful, students need to stretch their thinking. They may be inclined to resort to their first idea; teachers remind students that the goal is to identify an innovative response to a problem or situation. *Innovation* means to implement ideas to make them a reality or to add value to something. For example, 8th grade math students worked together in groups on the assignment described in Figure 5.3. In choosing what objects to use to represent variables, they considered what might make their demonstration innovative. One group chose cows and chickens as their variables and equated them with packages of meat at the grocery store. They created a graph and showed the relationships. The students succeeded in the assignment: not only did they demonstrate their understanding of the content, but they also chose a very innovative way to demonstrate qualities and quantities.

Designing Lessons to Target Creativity and Innovation

Figure 5.4 illustrates how to design a lesson to target creative thinking and innovation. This teacher is introducing a new unit that addresses the CCSS for interpreting informational texts and for speaking and listening, as well as the standard for evaluating or refining a technological solution that reduces impacts of human activities in natural systems. The teacher asks students to develop an innovative way to reverse the "greenhouse effect" so that it no longer worsens over time. For this lesson (which incorporates

FIGURE 5.3

Targeting Innovation Within Creative, Standards-Based Activities

CCSS Key Ideas and Details	Creative Activity Targeting Innovative Thinking
Ask and answer questions to demonstrate understanding of a text, referring explicitly to the text as the basis for the answers. (RL.3.1) Text: *Sarah, Plain and Tall* (MacLachlan, 1985)	Students develop a written description of a contextually appropriate innovation in response to the following prompt: *In the story* Sarah, Plain and Tall, *the Wittings live a simple life. Identify a need in the story that a character has and create an innovative tool to address the need.*
Quote accurately from a text when explaining what the text says explicitly and when drawing inferences from the text. (RL.5.1) Text: "Fog" (Sandburg, 1916)	Students develop a diagram or drawing and written description of an innovation that controls fog. The description includes references to the text that demonstrate how the innovation controls the different elements of fog described in the poem.
Use place value understanding to round decimals to any place. (5.NBT)	Students create an innovative design that teaches someone else the relationship between place value and decimals. They also describe their thinking through the five steps of the innovation process.
Create equations that describe numbers or relationships: Create equations in two or more variables to represent relationships between quantities; graph equations on coordinate axes with labels and scales. (HSA-CED.A.2)	Students use two or more objects that represent variables and come up with an innovative way to demonstrate the relationship between quantities. Their demonstration must include a description of their thinking through the five steps of the innovation process. They graph equations on coordinate axes with labels and scales.
Cite strong and thorough textual evidence to support analysis of what the text says explicitly as well as inferences drawn from the text, including determining where the text leaves matters uncertain. (RL.12.1) Text: Keats's "Ode on a Grecian Urn": "Beauty is truth, truth beauty,—that is all / Ye know on earth, and all ye need to know."	The urn in "Ode on a Grecian Urn" can be seen as an innovative idea. Students use the innovation process to analyze how the inspirational qualities of the urn resonated with Keats.

Note. CCSS = Common Core State Standards (National Governors Association Center for Best Practices, Council of Chief State School Officers, 2010a, 2010b).

FIGURE 5.4

Designing a Lesson: Targeting Creativity and Innovation

<table>
<tr><td>Identify Content, Topics, Subtopics, Skills, Concepts</td><td colspan="3">CCSS
• RI.9-10.1
• RI.9-10.2
• HS-ES53-4</td><td colspan="3">Topics:
• Sun's effect on climate
• Factors that affect climate
• Worldwide climate patterns</td><td colspan="3">Subtopics:
• Greenhouse effect
• Rotation, revolution
• Latitude
• Ocean currents
• Wind patterns
• Landforms
• El Niño</td><td colspan="3">Skills:
• Critical thinking
• Cause and effect
• Creative thinking: innovation and fluency
• Descriptive writing/wording</td></tr>
<tr><td>Essential Question</td><td colspan="12">How do human decisions affect climate?</td></tr>
<tr><td>Assessment</td><td colspan="12">Summative: rubric</td></tr>
<tr><td>Differentiation</td><td colspan="4">Ability
Reading: different reading levels</td><td colspan="4">Interest
No differentiation</td><td colspan="4">Cognitive style
Record responses</td></tr>
<tr><td>"Hook" Student Interest</td><td colspan="12">Teacher lists yearly temperatures and precipitation of five unnamed U.S. cities. Students guess what cities they are and give reasons for their choices.</td></tr>
<tr><td>Lesson Set-Up</td><td colspan="4">Teacher reviews/extends content:
The teacher reviews with students how westerly winds affect weather. Students orally compare weather in cities with the same latitude and discuss what would happen to the three latitude zones if Earth tilted at 66 2/3°.</td><td colspan="4">Teacher reviews the thinking process:
The teacher reminds students of a previous lesson where they demonstrated creative and innovative thinking. Class reviews the five-step innovation process to guide their work. Students understand that the assignment requires innovative thinking and identifying an innovative solution.</td><td colspan="4">Teacher reviews the product form:
The product form will be the innovation process paper where students record their ideas. The teacher reviews the rubric to ensure students understand how they will be assessed. Class reviews the rubric, and teacher clarifies any confusion or misunderstanding. The teacher describes the talk show format.</td></tr>
</table>

FIGURE 5.4 — (*continued*)

Designing a Lesson: Targeting Creativity and Innovation		
The Activity	Introduction: The teacher tells students they will use their imagination and their factual knowledge to think of an innovative way to reverse the pattern causing the greenhouse effect. Groups of students explore two websites with information on the greenhouse effect and ideas or recommendations that have already been tried or implemented to try to minimize the effect. The teacher provides sites with easier reading levels for students who struggle in reading.	Procedures: After conducting research, student groups brainstorm reasons why the greenhouse effect is getting worse and ideas that might respond to each potential explanation. Students generate group criteria and individually evaluate the ideas using the "eliminate and defend" strategy to help them make a logical decision. Students independently conceptualize an innovation, write or record the steps required to make the innovation happen, and surmise who will support them and who will likely put up roadblocks. They imagine their innovation coming to fruition and present their possible results and any ideas for improvements to the class in a talk show format.
Assessment	The teacher assesses the innovation process by marking the rubric and makes specific comments to elaborate on feedback.	

innovative thinking), students must be able work collaboratively in groups; they also need to know what the greenhouse effect is, what causes it, its effects, and steps that have already been taken to reduce these effects.

When introducing this lesson, the teacher highlights the focus on innovation so that students will pay attention to it, and models the innovative process by showing them examples from a prior lesson that generated student innovations. The teacher also shares examples from real life to illustrate how someone takes an idea and turns it into an innovative idea or an innovation. The teacher explains that students will use the five-step innovative process to develop their innovations. Students work together to collect and share facts and to brainstorm ideas. (As previously noted, by working in a group, students will come up with more ideas than they would on their own.) The teacher makes sure the groups are heterogeneously mixed and that the student's personalities complement each other. In the second stage of the process, when students evaluate ideas, they work together to generate criteria using the Eliminate and Defend strategy (see "Grab and Go" Idea #33). Then they work on their own to decide on the one idea that they think is best. Each student conceptualizes their chosen idea and determines the steps needed to complete the innovation. They anticipate who could help them with their innovation and who might be the naysayers. The final stage in this activity is a "talk show" (based on "Grab and Go" Idea #35) where students ask and answer questions about each other's innovation. In addition to discussing their idea with a partner, students write their responses to the questions.

The rubric for this assignment (see Figure 5.5) provides guidance to students and also a basis for teacher feedback for group and individual work. The rubric incorporates expected levels of creative thinking (fluency) and innovation. The teacher includes a self-assessment component because she wants students to understand how important it is for them to learn from

FIGURE 5.5

Sample Rubric for Lesson Targeting Creativity and Innovation

Assignment Element	Not So Hot	Okay	Very Good	Great
Group Assessment				
Brainstorm: Earth-sun relationships Rotation Revolution Greenhouse effect	Few facts Little or no evidence of research Facts only Little detail	Some facts Some evidence of research Facts with few additional imagined details Some detail	Many facts Evidence of research Facts combined with one or two original ideas Many details	Many facts Evidence of extensive research Facts combined with many original, logical ideas that enhance the scenario
Brainstorm solutions to the effects	One effect One solution	Two effects One or two solutions for one or two effects	Three effects Two solutions for each effect	More than three effects Three or more solutions for each effect
Individual Assessment				
Decision	No criteria applied in making decision	Obvious criteria applied in making decision	Most criteria applied in making decision	All criteria applied in making decision
Plan	Steps do not represent the innovation process Enablers and disablers incorrect or not listed	Some steps missing Obvious enablers and disablers listed	Steps are sequenced correctly with basic descriptions and make sense List of enablers and disablers makes sense and represents realistic ideas	Steps are sequenced correctly and are very descriptive and logical List of enablers and disablers makes sense and represents deep thinking
"Talk show" responses (written)	Some responses missing Some ideas not relevant	Responses are minimal Some ideas logical but not significant	Responses are complete Ideas are relevant and logical	Well-developed responses include specific details, thoughtful generalizations, and conclusions

their own self-evaluation and not solely rely on someone else's opinion of their work.

Providing students with feedback helps them become more effective innovative thinkers (see discussion in Chapter 7). When providing feedback, recognize students for the strengths they demonstrate within the innovation process and provide strategies and tips on how to improve in areas in which they are weak. The feedback is not about whether the student is a "good" innovative thinker, but rather how well students use fluent, flexible, original, and elaborative thinking in the different stages of the innovative process. Feedback should also address effort and how well students use critical thinking in order to converge their ideas.

Figure 5.6 sums up the tips for creating a classroom community that embraces an innovation mindset. The five different ways to promote an innovation mindset lay the foundation necessary for students to understand what innovation really is.

The more that students engage in innovation activities in school, the more they will begin to really understand innovation and the importance of it. Innovation does not apply to everything; there is a time and a place to innovate. When students use the innovative process, they learn the importance of developing a plan for implementation and how to direct their actions. Students will think of themselves as innovators if you ask them if they used innovative thinking today. Remind them that we evaluate the effects of our innovation because we value it.

The four "grab and go" strategies at the end of this chapter target the five steps of the innovative process. Within each step, students use one or more of their creative thinking skills (i.e., fluency, flexibility, originality, elaboration). They use divergent thinking when generating or considering more than one idea, and they use convergent thinking to decide upon the best idea. The actual innovative process as it is described in this chapter is procedural and can be found on Creativity Road 3. The "grab and go" strategies that are used in the different steps in the process are often found on Creativity Road 2.

FIGURE 5.6

Supporting Innovative Thinking: Tips for Success	
Tip	**How to Get There**
Build an innovative mindset	Provide a context Create an innovative climate Foster creativity Involve students in shared learning Measure success
Understand innovation	Have a common definition for teacher and students Put ideas into practice Understand the importance and relevance of innovation Know where to innovate
Plan for innovation	Model the process Identify who does what, when
Make innovation happen	Find ideas Analyze options Choose an idea Implement the ideas Manage the process Review results Share ideas

Reflecting on and Extending Chapter Information

1. Practically speaking, do you agree that using the innovation process can help students achieve the Common Core State Standards (or your individual state standards) in your content area? Elaborate.
2. Is there a place for innovation in our schools? Why or why not?
3. Do you think innovation needs to be differentiated for young students? Explain.

4. Describe how you would manage the class while they were engaged in an innovation lesson.
5. How would you compare lessons that emphasize creativity, imagination, and innovation to those that focus more on critical thinking?

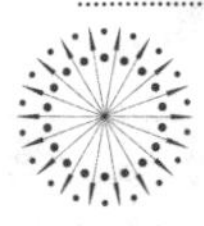

"Grab and Go" Idea #32

Nervous Nellie

The Nervous Nellie strategy (Creativity Road 2) promotes innovative thinking by having groups of students generate many different worries about a situation—and then generate many different ways to resolve these problems. It is designed to support students in the first step of the process of innovation (i.e., identify the need) and incorporates divergent thinking, fluency, and flexibility.

For example, 5th grade students studying western migration are told to place themselves in the role of Nervous Nellie, who is worried about going on the Conestoga wagon. Groups of students generate a list of Nellie's worries and categorize them by type of concern (see Figure 5.7). In this lesson, the first worry students identify is that it is dangerous. The category of concern that this worry falls into is safety.

The next step is for the team to identify the greatest need generated from the Nervous Nellie categories. Students tend to count the number of ideas listed in a category and mistakenly think the category that has the most ideas must represent the greatest need. This is the time to remind students to use flexible thinking. After identifying the different categories, students

1. Write all the categories on different index cards, mix them up, and place them face down on the table.
2. Choose someone from their group to record responses.
3. "Roll and respond": The recorder turns over a category card face up and rolls the dice. The student who has the number

on the dice must come up with an idea that will solve the worry category identified on the card.

4. The student who responded rolls the dice, and the student who has the number on the dice adds a solution or changes the category by flipping over the next card.
5. The recorder writes down all responses.

This process continues until the group has generated multiple different responses to all of Nellie's categories of worries.

FIGURE 5.7

Nervous Nellie: Innovative Thinking Strategy

Nellie's Worries	Type of Concern
It's dangerous.	Safety
There is not enough food.	Food
It is a very long trip.	Time
I don't like the leader.	Leadership
It is the wrong time of year.	Time
My friends are not going.	Companionship
I can't bring my dog.	Companionship
I am not comfortable.	Physical comfort
I can't get up on and down off the wagon.	Physical ability
I don't get along with some of the people.	Socialization

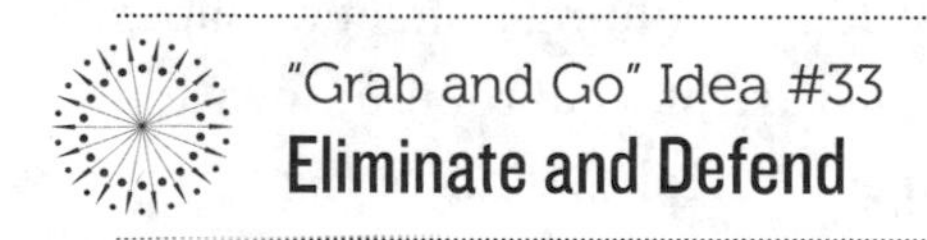

"Grab and Go" Idea #33

Eliminate and Defend

This Creativity Road 2 strategy helps students identify and choose their best idea (the second step in the innovative thinking process).

The class as a whole generates criteria to use to guide them in making a logical decision.

Questions that may be used to assess the validity of an innovative idea include the following:

- Is it practical?
- Is it appropriate (to the context, content, or topic)?
- Is it effective? Will it work?
- Is it long lasting?
- Is it reasonable? Is there time and are there materials?
- Is it innovative?

Based on the agreed-upon criteria, students, as a whole group, as a small group, or individually, compare two ideas at a time to eliminate the weaker idea. For each idea, they should identify which of the criteria is met or not met. Then, through a process of elimination (i.e., the stronger idea is compared to the next idea), students identify the final, best solution.

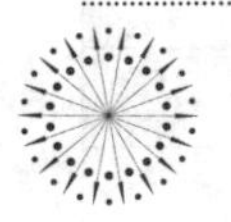

"Grab and Go" Idea #34

Creating Consensus

This Creativity Road 2 strategy asks students to visually develop their innovation. Students work collaboratively to help each other identify steps to move each student's innovation from an idea to full conceptualization. This small-group activity focuses on the third and fourth steps of the innovation process.

The activity begins with students folding a sheet of paper into eight squares. They draw one picture of what their innovation looks like in the first square. Each student shows his or her drawing to the group and explains it. At this point, other students in the group can ask questions about the innovation. After the discussion, the student writes in the second box what needs to be done first in order to make this innovation happen. Then the student passes the paper to the next student, who writes in the next box what should happen second. The students pass the papers around the table until the innovation process is complete. They can use the back side of the paper if they need extra space. If you are doing this with young students, you might want your students to fold the paper in fourths and list only four steps.

When students receive their papers back, they circle any ideas they had not thought of. Each student finalizes the steps to produce his or her own innovation and present it to the group. They include who can assist with the innovation and who might resist it. Then, as a group, they discuss the best ideas in order to form a consensual innovation solution. When students feel they have addressed all potential challenges, they are ready to submit their innovation and the innovation process to the teacher.

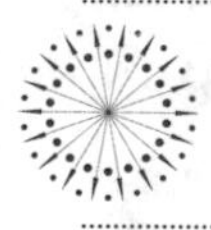

"Grab and Go" Idea #35

Talk Show

This Creativity Road 2 strategy allows students to self-assess their innovation and addresses the final stage in the innovative process. Students work in pairs; one student is the talk show "host," who will ask preset questions regarding the student's innovation, and the other student is the "guest." The host does not know what the guest's answers will be. The host is allowed to ask the guest to elaborate or clarify. All students review the questions ahead of time and write their responses; they can refer to this work during the talk show but should not simply read them aloud. Examples of questions include the following:

1. What was the purpose of this assignment?
2. How did your innovative idea meet the purpose of the assignment?

3. What did you learn from using the innovative process?
4. By doing this project, did you learn any strategies to improve your thinking and learning? If so, what were they, and how do they apply to innovation?
5. What did you learn about yourself as a team member? Be specific and give examples.
6. If you could change anything about this assignment, what would it be and why?
7. Do you have anything else you would like to add?

Pairs of students trade places and repeat the process. When the interviews are complete, students turn in their responses to the teacher. Students reflect on their own learning using the assignment rubric. The class should also discuss the assignment as a whole, sharing what they learned and their responses to the questions.

Teachers can expand upon this idea by having students develop content-based questions for each other, by video recording the interviews or performing them in class, by having the "host" ask follow-up questions, or by having the talk show "hosts" also assess their "guests" using the assignment rubric.

Creativity and Problem Solving

Working It Out Creatively

Creative problem solving is necessary when there is a discrepancy between what exists and the desired situation. It often involves finding a solution that is either unknown or not commonly used. Students use creative problem solving skills when developing original ideas, creating innovations, and improving their own products. Like other areas of creativity, creative problem solving can be used to help students think more deeply about content.

Noller (1979) defined *creative problem solving* as

> having an element of newness and being relevant. By problem we mean: any situation which presents a challenge, offers an opportunity, or is a concern. By solving we mean: devising ways to answer or to meet or satisfy the problem. (pp. 4–5)

Torok (n.d.) identified two types of problems that require solving: acute problems and chronic problems. *Acute problems* need immediate attention—and *chronic problems* will turn into acute problems if they are ignored. There are also *anticipatory problems;* these "what if" problems are commonly explored in the creative classroom, and they provide students the opportunity to explore content deeply:

- Anticipatory problems ask students to consider an existing problem and make it bigger. For example, in some parts of the world, there is a water shortage. Scientists predict that the water shortage will become widespread in the not-too-distant future. Students are given a problem-based situation such as, "Imagine the year is 2025 and there is a worldwide water shortage. There is not enough drinking water for everyone on the planet." Students then use creative problem solving skills to solve the problem.
- Anticipatory problems require students to reflect upon the causes or effects of a situation. This may include retrospection, wherein students reflect upon a past problem and solution and create a different solution. In reading, for example, the student identifies a problem in the story and the solution the author has provided, then uses the creative problem solving process to develop a solution that improves upon the original one.

Students use the creative problem solving process in *problem-based learning* to help them solve problems. The research on problem-based learning indicates positive outcomes in the areas of student content knowledge, collaborative skills, engagement and motivation, and critical thinking and problem solving skills (University of Indianapolis Center of Excellence in Leadership of Learning, 2009). In problem-based learning, groups of students may solve problems following a process that requires them to take a particular point of view. Teachers facilitate the process, but students take increasing responsibility as they work through the different stages of problem solving. Students using this process "learn at least as much as traditionally instructed students" (Karnes & Bean, 2009, p. 309). Evidence also suggests that student achievement increases as students become more independently self-directed (van de Hurk, 2006, as cited in Karnes & Bean, 2009, p. 310).

There are other models and methods of problem solving. Gordon (1961) developed Synectics, a method of applying analogies to promote creative thinking and creative problem solving. Synectics helps students generate unusual connections that they apply to solving a problem. Although fairly common in the business world as a strategy for coming up with new or improved products, this approach is less commonly seen in the education setting. Synectics includes four types of analogies:

1. *Direct analogies* compare a topic, concept, or even a person to a living thing or to an inanimate object (see McAuliffe & Stoskin, 1993). For example, "In what ways are decimals like a dog?" or "In what ways are decimals like a box?"
2. *Personal analogies* promote identifying emotionally with the topic or concept. One type of personal analogy is a first-person description of facts that usually lacks emotion (e.g., "I am decimal and I have a decimal point. I affect place value. I make it easy to see quantities less than one."). The second type of personal analogy is to describe the topic or concept with emotion (e.g., "I am a decimal and I am happy when I have lots of whole numbers because then I feel big. I am sad when I am not even equal to one."). The third type of personal analogy is empathic identification with a person, animal, or inanimate object (e.g., "I am a decimal and I can frustrate students when there are lots of us. I am a decimal and I make students happy when they manipulate my numbers rather than manipulate the numbers in fractions.").

3. *Symbolic analogies* (also known as the *compressed conflict stage*) identify two conflicting aspects of the analogy and place them together. For example, in Maine, we use the expression "wicked good" when something is very good. Other examples of symbolic analogies are "organized mess, imaginary reality, doubtful certainty, and destructive construction" (McAuliffe & Stoskin, 1993, p. 111). With our decimal example, students can respond to "In what ways are decimals simply complex?"
4. *Fantasy* uses the ideas from the previous analogies to generate a "what if" solution (e.g., "What if dividing decimals were easy?").

In his early work, Osborn (1963) described the problem solving process as comprising fact finding, idea finding, and solution finding. This idea evolved to include problem finding and acceptance finding (i.e., implementation) and, later, a balance between convergent and divergent thinking in each stage of the problem solving process. Now known as the Osborn-Parnes Creative Problem Solving (CPS) model (Parnes, 1992), each of the five steps (i.e., fact finding, problem finding, idea finding, solution finding, acceptance finding) includes a divergent thinking phase (e.g., brainstorming) and a convergent thinking phase. According to Treffinger, Isaksen, and Stead-Dorval (2006), the CPS model can be distilled into three components: understanding the problem, generating ideas, and planning for action.

Encouraging Creative Problem Solving

To be successful in creative problem solving, students must be able to cope with ambiguity. Many problems are posed in "fuzzy" situations. Students must be comfortable sorting through the information that is given, exploring information that is not explicit but implied, and making informed decisions along the way. If students are frustrated with ambiguity, they will have a difficult time deconstructing the problem scenario. So, as with other creative thinking skills, teachers may need to model for students how to move forward when faced with ambiguous situations and problems. It is helpful for students to identify the nouns (e.g., who is involved in the problem scenario and what the apparent problem is) and identify the verb that will direct the action. Students adept in problem analysis are able to determine if their solution to the ambiguous situation is the best possible solution. They recognize that periods of uncertainty may occur before they are able to determine the outcome.

The creative problem solving process is driven by curiosity, which compels discovery of data, opportunities, and solutions. If students lack curiosity, they may be unable to effectively define and redefine problems. You can pique students' curiosity by using question stems that spark their interest.

The creative problem solving process is also driven by students' confidence. This characteristic enables students to express a different idea and proceed quickly through each step of the process.

Creative thinking requires suspending judgment. In the idea-generating stage, it can be helpful to remind students that the rules of brainstorming include suspending judgments. Students will use convergent thinking, which requires judgment, later in the process to determine which problem is the overarching problem and which solution is the most effective solution. Creative problem solvers need to be able to perceive bias and prejudice to avoid falling prey to false conclusions based upon prejudicial reasoning. Although we can teach students the skills of identifying bias and prejudice, it is much more difficult to teach them how to resist the peer pressure that can also lead students to false conclusions. Empowering students to become effective, creative problem solvers gives them a tool in resisting group conformity.

Helping students develop as creative problem solvers gives them a valuable survival skill for their future education, careers, and citizenship. It is important for students to be able to ask the right questions and solve the right problems, creatively. To create an environment conducive to creative problem solving,

- *Expose students to the creative problem solving process.* Take the time to teach students a creative problem solving process that is age appropriate and language friendly. Demonstrate how to use the framework and when to use it, regularly providing students with lessons that require creative problem solving. Encourage students to identify when they need to use the creative problem solving process and when it is not necessary.
- *Help students learn to manage their time.* Remind them that the creative problem solving process may be used to analyze information and be completed in one class period, or it may involve a process that takes days, weeks, or months to complete.
- *Provide visual illustrations of the steps in the creative problem solving process.* This can be a poster in the classroom or a document that is shared on Google Docs or a class website.
- *Ensure that the classroom environment values creative ideas and solutions.* In creative problem solving, ideas and solutions that may appear off track should still be explored for further consideration. Ideas and solutions may be modified or ultimately may be considered wrong. As with other types of creative thinking, "wrong" does not mean the student has failed in the creative problem solving process.
- *Use creative problem solving as a tool to promote achievement and foster intellectual curiosity.* The creative problem solving process is not a "what"; it is a "how." The curriculum and standards identify *what* teachers are to teach. *How* we teach content, however, is up to us.

Defining the Creative Problem Solving Process

The creative problem solving process (in Creativity Road 3) I like to use combines ideas from several different models. The process includes three major parts—the problem, the solution, and implementation of the solution—each of which is broken down into a series of steps (see Figure 6.1). This model is appropriate for both independent and group problem solving, and each part of the process includes both divergent and convergent thinking. This process also includes student reflection and self-assessment at two points: after the first two parts (identifying problems and identifying solutions) and at the completion of the process. The importance of this reflection is twofold: asking students to examine their thought processes during the activity builds a metacognitive awareness of the problem solving process and creative skills, and student self-assessment promotes autonomy in the learning process, which improves student performance (Jensen, 2013). The model may be modified by simplifying a step or by making a step more complex; steps may be eliminated in order to align the model with content and the student needs. However, there are core non-negotiable steps in the process that should remain constant.

Part I: The Problem

The first step in the process is for students to list what they do not know, what they think they know, and what they definitely know about the problem. To support this type of divergent thinking, teachers can either provide students with a chart to fill in or fold a paper into thirds, creating three columns to list their responses. At this point, students should be sorting facts from information they need to research; the activity also gives them an early inkling as to the problem or problems.

Teachers who prefer to use a more interactive strategy play a brainstorming game (Creativity Road 2): "I've got the question; who knows the problem?" Through discussion, the class generates

FIGURE 6.1

The Creative Problem Solving Process

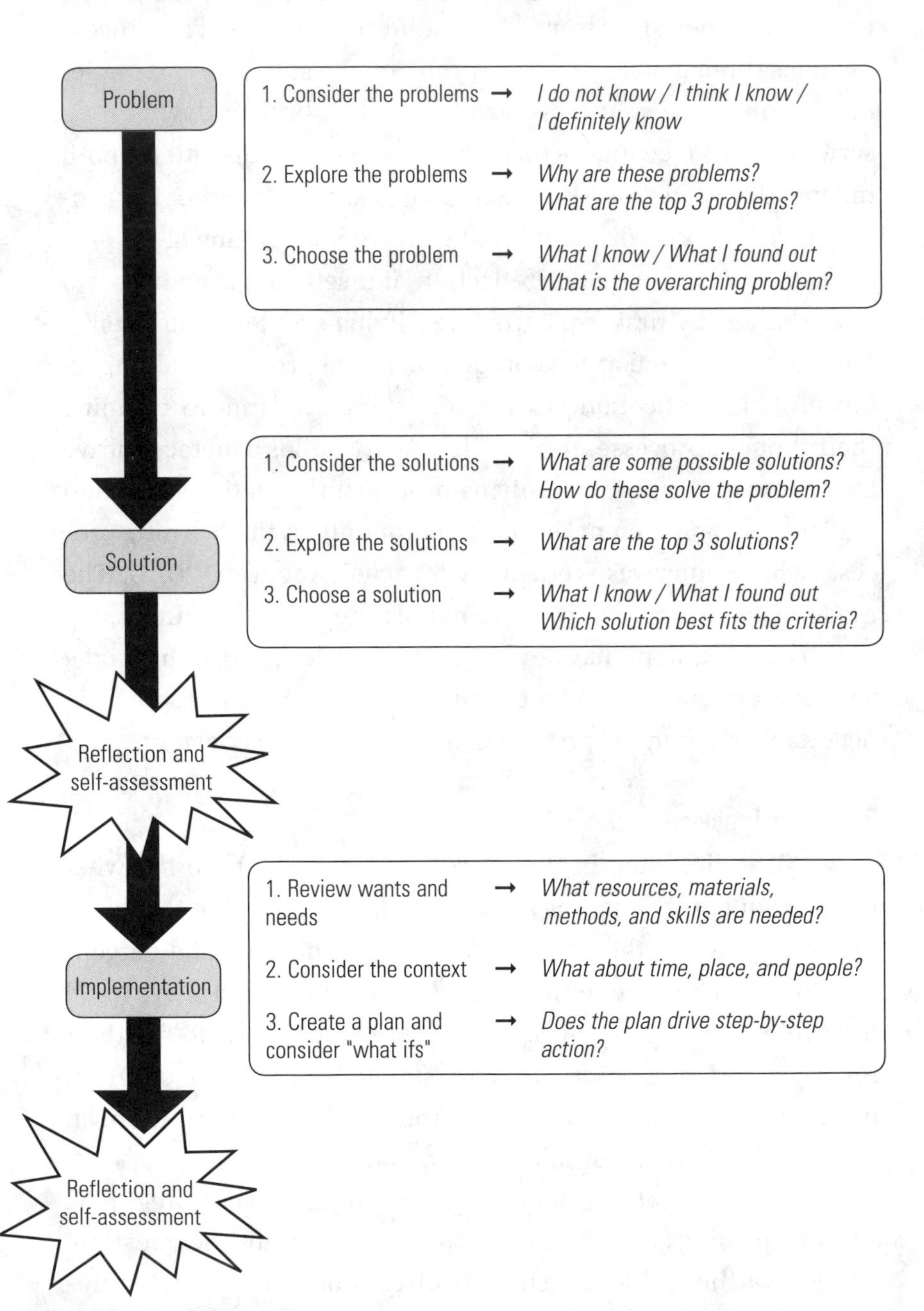

a series of questions about the topic—for example, "How can the people in the town of Chew and Swallow stop the food from falling from the sky?" (see Barrett & Barrett, 1978). Then, students individually identify problems based upon the questions (e.g., "The town smells bad."); they share their problem with the class, and the other students guess which question matches the problem.

Once students have identified multiple problems, they identify which problem is most significant, or which is the overarching or underlying problem. To do this, they narrow down their list of possibilities to the three most significant. One way to help them with this process is to have students create a concept web generating reasons why each is a problem. This should help them recognize common themes among the different ideas. After identifying their top three possibilities, students conduct research to help identify the "real" problem (i.e., overarching or most important).

Students may need support in developing the ability to determine which of the three problems is most significant; again, a class Creative Road 2 activity can help guide them to distinguishing between problems that are "really big" and those that are just "kind of big." This can be done using the three problems as headings on chart paper or by moving text around on an interactive whiteboard. Students identify what they know about each problem and conduct research to elaborate on their ideas. As they gain information, they add sticky information to the appropriate column. After they compare their information on each problem, they identify the overarching problem. To help students summarize and compare information, teachers can provide a simple template for them to fill in. Figure 6.2 illustrates a student's use of a template guiding identification of the overarching problem in the fairy tale *Cinderella*.

In this part of the process, the nonnegotiable is for students to consider all the related problems before deciding which is the overarching or underlying problem. When students are asked to identify a problem, they often choose one that is apparent—and sometimes this is not the actual problem. If they seek and find a solution to the apparent problem, this may not necessarily solve the real problem or resolve the situation, because they have not addressed the overarching essential problem. It's like dealing with a symptom without dealing with the cause: if the cause is not dealt with, the symptom often reappears. Therefore, teachers using the problem solving process in the classroom must require students

FIGURE 6.2

Investigating Problems

Problem #1 Cinderella wants to go to the ball.	Problem #2 The stepmother does not want her to go to the ball.	Problem #3 Cinderella is poor.
What I know	**What I know**	**What I know**
She wants to meet the prince.	*The stepmother is mean.*	*Cinderella was born a peasant.*
She thinks it will be fun.	*The stepmother is jealous of Cinderella.*	*Her father did not have much money.*
She has never been to a ball before.	*The stepmother wants her daughters to meet the prince.*	*The stepmother does not share her money with Cinderella.*
What I found out	**What I found out**	**What I found out**
Not all balls end up fun.	*Stepmothers are often unhappy in fairy tales.*	*Poor people often end up happy in fairy tales.*
Balls are full of rich socialites.	*Stepmothers are often the bad person in fairy tales.*	*The use of magic and trickery often turns the problem around in fairy tales.*
Women go to balls to meet rich men.		*Poor people are often nice in fairy tales.*
Balls only happen once in a while.		*Poor people are often the victim in fairy tales.*
After reviewing what I know and what I found out, I decided that the really big problem is: *Cinderella is poor. This problem affects all the other problems.*		

to consider other problems before determining which is the overarching "real" problem.

Part 2: The Solution

In the first step of this part of the process, students generate many solutions to the overarching problem, identify how each solution will solve the problem, and then review the information and choose the three best solutions. Again, the brainstorming process (Creativity Road 2) can be done as a group activity. For example, the class divides into small groups, each of which has a set of numbered playing cards (teachers can limit the cards to ace through six); individual students suggest a number of solutions based on the number on the card they are dealt. After assessing and evaluating the different possibilities, students choose the top three potential solutions to research. They research information about each of the three possible solutions to make sure that they have enough information about each to make an informed choice.

In choosing the best solution, students generate criteria against which to measure their ideas; individual criteria also should be weighted for importance and impact. For example, to revisit solving Cinderella's dilemma, our student has decided that the three best solutions to the problem of being poor are for Cinderella to find a lot of money, for a fairy godmother to work magic, or for Cinderella to take assertiveness training. Figure 6.3 illustrates the student's assessment of these possible solutions and selection of the best, per her criteria. Criteria are the critical elements behind making an informed decision. Since this is such a difficult skill for students, teachers use gradual release of responsibility (Fisher & Frey, 2012) to wean students toward independence. First, teachers provide criteria appropriate for the decision. In subsequent lessons, the teacher provides some criteria and students add to them until students are ready to generate appropriate, effective criteria on their own.

FIGURE 6.3

Evaluating Solutions

Directions: Rank each of your top 3 solutions on a scale of 1–10 on the basis of your criteria.

Indicate which of your criteria is the most important by shading the box for that heading.

Then, total the points for each possible solution. Do not assume the highest number is the best choice; remember that you have selected one criterion as most important.

In the bottom box, identify which solution you are choosing and why.

Possible criteria: cost, practicality, realistic, materials, manpower, long lasting. You may also develop your own criteria.

Solutions	Criteria				Total score
	Long lasting	*Fast results*	*Effective*	*Interesting*	
A great deal of gold	*8*	*10*	*7*	*3*	*28*
Fairy godmother fixes all	*6*	*8*	*7*	*7*	*28*
Assertiveness training	*5*	*3*	*9*	*10*	*27*

The solution I think is best is: *For Cinderella to take assertiveness training.*

Because: *My most important criteria was that the solution be interesting because this is a fairy tale. I think it would be interesting for Cinderella to do assertiveness training. She will use her new skills to find a job.*

Another way to ensure that students are understanding the process and acquiring problem solving skills is to have them generate as many reasons as they can to defend their solutions. For younger students and those new to the process, sharing ideas in a class discussion and then coaching students to a consensus may help them in skill development.

This part of the problem solving process has two nonnegotiable steps. One is for students to consider many solutions. Often, students want to use the first solution that comes to mind or a solution that is most interesting to them. It is important for students to use creative flexible thinking to come up with many solutions. Even far-out solutions are useful here, because they may lead students to more realistic solutions. If students are going to take the time to really creatively problem solve, then the problem must be important enough to establish criteria to help them select the best solution. This step is also nonnegotiable.

Time Out: Reflection

After the first two parts of the problem solving process have been completed, my model includes a pause for reflection and self-assessment. This is a chance for both students and teacher to evaluate the quality of the responses in the preceding steps. The pause for reflection is an important part of the creative problem solving process. Before students go on to make a plan for implementing their solution, they need to assess how well they applied the process. This offers them the opportunity to revise or improve their responses—and improve their problem solving skills. Teachers can develop a worksheet to guide student self-reflection, including questions such as the following:

- Did I list all the problems I could think of?
- Did I fully explain why each problem was a problem?
- What did I do to learn more about each problem?
- Did I choose the most significant problem?
- Did I use flexible thinking in coming up with solutions?
- Did I explain how each solution responded to the problem?
- How well did my criteria identify sensible and helpful solutions?
- How did I make my decision about which solution to choose?
- Did I do quality work? Why or why not? If not, what can I do to revise and improve my work?

Teachers can enhance student thinking and reflecting through prompts using the words *why* and *how*. For example, ask, "How do you know you did your best thinking in this process so far?" When the student responds, follow up with "Why did you...?" This can guide students to more carefully consider the process and their performance.

There is no point in spending time designing an implementation plan if the solution is not the best solution. Students are used to evaluation occurring at the end of a process and may not recognize this step as important, but it is nonnegotiable. This step gives students the chance to revise their work and revisit their decisions before completing the process.

Part 3: Implementation

In the third part of the problem solving process, students consider what resources, materials, methods, and skills will enable successful implementation of their solution. Students fold a paper into fourths and write each requirement category on the top of the column. They use divergent thinking to brainstorm ideas about each topic and place them in the correct column. They use convergent thinking when they organize their ideas in each column from extremely important to not so important. Students make sure their most important ideas end up in their final plan.

In the second step of the implementation stage, students consider context: they create three webs and brainstorm ideas associated with time, place, and people. Highlighting the most significant ideas from each web compels students to consider where they will include or account for this information in their implementation plan.

Finally, students transform their ideas into action plans. The plan for implementation specifies what is required for realization: the steps that need to be taken, and when; who might be responsible for different aspects, and what they need to do; and anything else that will enable successful implementation (e.g., materials, funding). The plan also should help students assess their progress toward their goal. Regardless of whether plans are actually carried out (e.g., students build a model or conduct an experiment) or just imagined, developing the plan allows students to see their solution played out.

As with previous parts of the process, teachers can develop templates or graphic organizers to help students manage developing and implementing their solutions. The detail of the plan itself and its presentation varies by content area and student age—and the teacher's time commitment for the overall unit. However, consider this step as an opportunity for additional creativity in the classroom by allowing students to produce a plan in a format other than writing. For example, young students could create digital stories explaining their solutions and implementation plans. For older students, a group problem solving assignment might include a multimedia presentation of their ideas and how to implement their solution. Turning the solution into an implementation plan is nonnegotiable. This is where students discover why their solution will or will not work (and if not, why it may need to be modified): the validation of their problem solving.

Reflection and Self-Assessment

At the end of the process, students reflect and self-assess. They evaluate the formulation of their plan, how well they solved the problem, and whether they communicated their idea effectively. This reflection also gives the teacher an opportunity to provide feedback and insight. A joint teacher-student evaluation (see Figure 6.4 for an example) should be based, of course, on guidelines previously provided to students.

FIGURE 6.4

Creative Problem Solving Process Evaluation

Teacher Evaluation				
Category	Not so much	Good	Very good	WOW!!
The solution is detailed.				
The solution is well thought out.				
The solution appears to solve the problem.				
The solution is effectively communicated to an audience.				
Teacher comments:				

Student Self-evaluation				
Category	Not so much	Good	Very good	WOW!!
The solution is detailed.				
The solution is well thought out.				
The solution appears to solve the problem.				
The solution is effectively communicated to an audience.				
What I like best about my solution and my work on the project: What I would do differently: What makes this "over the top":				

Applying Creative Problem Solving Across Content Areas

Creative problem solving can be applied to any content. In every content area there are issues to be addressed and problems to solve:

- *In a literacy unit,* creative problem solving helps students achieve a deeper understanding. Using the structure created by the author, the reader learns to hunt for details and see patterns within texts (and draw conclusions from them) in order to solve problems in a story. Readers make connections between characters and events—and often to their own lives—through the problem solving process.
- *In math,* teachers can use creative problem solving to help students understand that meaning is made from numbers and operations. Problem-solving scenarios can help students understand a math concept, using either physical or abstract representations. Students can design and collect surveys, analyze data and share results, or create simulations and experiments and show relevant data in all three parts of the creative problem solving process.
- *In science,* creative problem solving supports students as they explore effects of water on Earth's surface, solve the problem of finite energy resources and our global demand for energy, or assess a species's chances for survival.
- *In social studies,* the process can be applied when studying government, history, geography, culture, and economics. Students solve problems related to rights and responsibilities and international relations when studying civics and government, think about "what ifs" in a history unit, or study how humans interact with their environment. In an economics unit, the teacher can use problem-based learning to pose a situation based on topics such as consumer economics, international trade, and global interdependence, and link these to situations involving personal decisions about money.

Targeting Creative Problem Solving Within Standards-Based Activities

Most "typical" lessons can be adapted to accommodate and incorporate creative problem solving. Figure 6.5 shows how the process can be included when addressing the same content standards that we have explored in previous chapters.

The problem posed in the high school literacy example is quite abstract. How can the figures painted on the urn be free from time and at the same time be frozen in time? What might the problem be for the figures, and how might this problem be solved? If students take this prompt seriously, the problem solving process can help them to think deeply and in a complex way about the human condition. Teachers can encourage deep thinking by including specific language for students to use as criteria when evaluating their solutions. Teachers also use criteria on a scoring rubric to evaluate the lesson based on logical reasoning and critical and creative thinking.

When using creative problem solving in math, teachers generally think about how they can require students to really show what they know about the math concept. In the 5th grade math example, the prompt mirrors a common question teachers hear from students in the math class: "Why do I have to know this?" Setting this up as a problem scenario helps students discover the relevance of a math concept to their own lives. The 8th grade example, similarly, relates content to students' lives and also demonstrates how a straight computation example can easily be changed into a problem-based lesson.

Because it generally takes a bit more time to work on a lesson that incorporates creative problem solving than for the typical lesson, teachers might choose to do this type of lesson once per unit. Any time spent including the process as part of classroom activities will benefit students.

FIGURE 6.5

Creative Problem Solving Within Standards-Based Activities

CCSS Key Ideas and Details	Creative Problem Solving Prompt and Product
Ask and answer questions to demonstrate understanding of a text, referring explicitly to the text as the basis for the answers. (RL.3.1) Text: *Sarah, Plain and Tall* (MacLachlan, 1985)	*In the story* Sarah, Plain and Tall, *solve Jacob's problem of not having a wife. Provide references to the text where possible.* Product: Creative problem solving templates and discussion
Quote accurately from a text when explaining what the text says explicitly and when drawing inferences from the text. (RL.5.1) Text: "Fog" (Sandburg, 1916)	*Solve the problem of the fog moving on.* Product: Creative problem solving templates and discussion
Use place value understanding to round decimals to any place. (5.NBT)	*Suzie does not understand why she needs to learn about place value. She knows how to use decimals; why does she need to know how decimals relate to place value? Determine whose problem this is and how to solve the problem.* Product: Creative problem solving templates
Create equations that describe numbers or relationships: Create equations in two or more variables to represent relationships between quantities; graph equations on coordinate axes with labels and scales. (HSA-CED.A.2)	*Janice likes to sleep late in the morning, and her brother likes to get up early in the morning. Their parents get up somewhere in between the two of them. This is causing a problem.* *Identify the problem and solve it. Because Janice's dad is a math professor, he wants to see this problem solved logically in terms of variables, graphics, and equations. Phew! That adds an extra challenge to this problem.* Product: Creative problem solving templates and related math graphs
Cite strong and thorough textual evidence to support analysis of what the text says explicitly as well as inferences drawn from the text, including determining where the text leaves matters uncertain. (RL.12.1) Text: Keats's "Ode on a Grecian Urn": "Beauty is truth, truth beauty,—that is all / Ye know on earth, and all ye need to know."	*Solve the problem of the human figures on the urn being free from time and frozen in time.* Product: Creative problem solving templates and discussion

Note: CCSS = Common Core State Standards (National Governors Association Center for Best Practices, Council of Chief State School Officers, 2010a, 2010b).

Designing Lessons to Target Creative Problem Solving

Although some lessons that incorporate creative problem solving can be completed in a single class period, if students are doing extensive research exploring problems and solutions, then teachers need to plan accordingly. Longer projects can result in students getting bogged down with the process (particularly those who typically are easily bored), so teachers may need to embed motivational techniques in the lesson to retain student interest. Students who do not like to write or have difficulty writing might be allowed to audio or video record their responses. Differentiating on the basis of student ability, interest, learning profile, and students' preferred cognitive style (see discussion in Chapter 1) helps maintain student engagement and motivation.

Figure 6.6 illustrates how to design a lesson to incorporate creative problem solving. In this case, 3rd grade students are using what they have learned in their weather unit to solve the problem of land destruction caused by hurricanes. They have learned about the different ways people have already tried to minimize the effects of hurricane damage. Now, they are expected to think creatively of a different way that may be more effective. The teacher hooks the students and sets the stage for the upcoming lesson by showing students a YouTube video (see Herby, 2005), and then by playing a game where students are "experts" on different aspects of hurricanes and respond to questions.

At this point, students are placed in groups and begin working together through the parts of the creative problem solving process. This particular lesson incorporates a digital storytelling project, which promotes collaborative work. Different students must take on (or be assigned) different roles in order to complete this part of the assignment efficiently. Some students work on the clip art, some write dialog and text, some deal with layout, and others practice orally presenting the group's solution. Students' final reflection and self-assessment includes a description of their individual role in the group project.

This same lesson can be adapted for completion in a single day, too. Instead of showing a video to hook students, the teacher shows one picture of hurricane devastation. Instead of playing "Ask the Expert," the class lists what students think they know and what they definitely know. Students brainstorm problems as the teacher records their ideas on the board, and then the class votes on the three best ideas. They brainstorm solutions and narrow their solutions down to three. The teacher provides two criteria, and students generate two more ideas. The class evaluates the solutions, settles on the best one, and generates an implementation plan. Students individually create digital stories during their literacy period (or as homework) demonstrating the solution to the problem, share their story with a classmate, and complete a self-assessment.

Creative problem solving is an important skill in school, in the workplace, and in life. Students will not necessarily consider overarching problems unless they are exposed to a model such as this one. If they do not practice the creative problem solving process, they are left on their own to discover that an apparent problem is not necessarily the problem that needs to be solved. If students are not reminded to stop and gather additional information before trying to solve a problem, many will not do this. If students do not brainstorm solutions before choosing one, they most likely will just choose the first solution that comes to mind. If students do not stop and reflect on their decisions before they implement them, many will just rush through to complete the task.

Not all problems warrant a step-by-step process. It is important for students to realize that creative problem solving is only helpful when they really need to think through a problem. When students use the process, they are actually reviewing content; they cannot effectively apply this process unless they know and understand the content. The creative problem solving process enables students to extend their thinking beyond the usual and the known, and requires them to use all of their creative thinking

FIGURE 6.6

Designing a Lesson: Creative Problem Solving

<table>
<tr><td>Identify Content, Topics, Subtopics, Skills, Concepts</td><td colspan="3">CCSS addressed:
• 3-ESS3-1
• RI.3.1
• RI.3.9
• W.3.1</td><td colspan="3">Topics:
• Weather conditions
• Weather instruments
• Weather prediction
• Severe weather</td><td colspan="3">Subtopics:
• Temperature
• Wind
• Clouds
• Precipitation
• Air pressure
• Humidity
• Condensation
• Evaporation
• Barometer
• Anemometer
• Atmosphere</td><td colspan="3">Skills:
• Critical thinking: cause and effect
• Creative problem solving
• Design engineering
• Digital storytelling</td></tr>
<tr><td>Essential Question</td><td colspan="12">Why is it important to understand the causes and effects of severe weather?</td></tr>
<tr><td>Assessment</td><td colspan="12">Summative: rubric, self-assessment</td></tr>
<tr><td>Differentiation</td><td colspan="4">Ability
Internet resource with lower readability levels
Modified number of problem-solving steps</td><td colspan="4">Interest
Technology: digital storytelling</td><td colspan="4">Cognitive style
Use of images</td></tr>
<tr><td>"Hook" Student Interest</td><td colspan="12">The teacher shows students a YouTube video about Hurricane Katrina (Herby, 2005).
The class plays "I've got the answer; who has the question?" to review content information.</td></tr>
</table>

FIGURE 6.6 — (*continued*)

Designing a Lesson: Creative Problem Solving

Lesson Set-Up	Teacher reviews/extends content: The teacher reviews with students how wind, precipitation, and tides affect land during a hurricane.	Teacher reviews the thinking process: The teacher reminds students of a previous lesson where they used the creative problem solving process, and tells them they will be using this process again to help them solve the problem of the effects of hurricane damage to land.	Teacher reviews the product form: The teacher shows students the product form: problem solving templates and a digital story describing or showing their solution. The teacher reviews with students the rubric that will help them assess their work and responds to any questions regarding expectations.
The Activity	Introduction and Procedures, Day 1: Groups of students develop problem concept webs based on information they learn from websites identified by the teacher. Students are expected to reference the website and their science book as they work through the creative problem solving process. On Day 1 they are expected to complete the concept web and identify the overarching problem. The teacher tells students they will use the creative problem solving process to solve the problem of land destruction caused by a hurricane.	Procedures, Day 2: Groups continue their work, brainstorming and researching solutions to the problems they identified on Day 1. They apply criteria and select the solution to the problem. Students pause and reflect on their work, discussing the problem solving process and making any adjustments needed to their templates.	
	Procedures, Day 3: Groups develop an implementation plan for their solution, and then develop a presentation on their solution using a digital storytelling format.	Procedures, Day 4: Groups present their solutions to the class and respond to questions.	
Assessment	Students complete a self-assessment based on the project rubric, then meet with the teacher to discuss their performance and receive feedback.		

Note. Reading and writing standards are from the Common Core State Standards (National Governors Association Center for Best Practices, Council of Chief State School Officers, 2010a); science standard is from the Next Generation Science Standards (NGSS Lead States, 2013).

skills (i.e., fluency, flexibility, originality, elaboration). They must be able to move back and forth between divergent thinking and convergent thinking. By participating in and practicing this process, students come to understand that creative problem solving is a logical, rational process that can benefit themselves and others.

Both of the "grab and go" activities at the end of this chapter can be used in either the first or second part of the creative problem solving process. Many of the "grab and go" activities included in the other chapters could be used here as well; just because a particular strategy is placed in a particular chapter does not mean it cannot be used in a different context.

Reflecting on and Extending Chapter Information

1. Describe the differences between decision making, problem solving, and creative problem solving. When would you use each one?
2. Should all students be required to learn and be able to use a creative problem solving process in school? Why or why not?
3. Do you see value in teaching a life skill such as creative problem solving within your content area? If so, do you believe this type of activity can also address the curriculum standards you use?
4. Why is it important to not just use creative problem solving in a lesson but also address the process metacognitively?
5. Do you think the innovative process and the creative problem solving processes that are procedural in nature (Creativity Road 3) are more effective in promoting creative thinking than the individual strategies that are emphasized on Creativity Road 2? Why or why not?

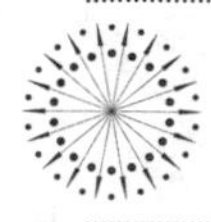

"Grab and Go" Idea #36

Generating Question Prompts

As with other "grab and go" prompting ideas, using specific questioning can help students in either the first or second part of the creative problem solving process. This Creativity Road 2 strategy can be used to brainstorm problems or solutions. This activity requires students to develop questions relating to the content. The teacher provides generic questions such as the following:

- What does this problem (or solution) mean to different people?
- What sources of information do I have that will help to inform me about this problem (or solution)?
- What has already been tried?
- What grabs my attention about this problem (or solution)?
- What questions do I have about this problem (or solution)?
- What might get in the way of solving this problem (or solution)?

Students take the generic questions and make them content-specific. For example, "What does this problem mean to different people?" changes to "What does the pollution problem mean to the scientist, the consumer, or the automobile maker?" Students continue to transpose the generic questions to come up with as many content-specific questions as possible. It is only through sifting through a multitude of possibilities that we can see patterns and identify relationships. When brainstorming, students let their imaginations soar.

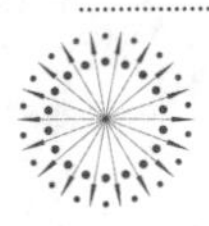

"Grab and Go" Idea #37

You Be the Judge

This Creativity Road 2 activity supports students' skill in narrowing down possibilities to make the best choice. It is a whole-class activity that provides an opportunity for students to process their decision in the first or second stage of the creative problem solving process.

When identifying problems or solutions via class discussion, the class narrows down the top three choices to two choices. The teacher divides the class in half. Half of the class defends one choice and half of the class the other. Each side is then broken down further into groups of four. Each group of four lists their reasons why they believe their problem is the overarching problem, or why their solution is the best one. Once their reasons are listed, students order their reasons from most to least significant. When time is up, the teacher identifies a student from one side to present the one best reason, and then the other side does the same, until each group of four has presented at least two or three ideas. At the end of the time, the student judge selects the best answer based upon both the number of responses for the same reason and the depth of reasoning (criteria). The losing side can appeal the decision, in which case the judge must defend his or her decision. If an argument breaks out, the decision moves to the "Supreme Court justice," the teacher.

Creativity and Assessment

Realizing What Counts

Does assessment kill creativity? "It depends" (Beghetto, 2005, p. 255). We can use assessment and feedback in our efforts to make creativity intentional in our classrooms (Kaufman, Plucker, & Baer, 2008). We do this by identifying the creative thinking part of the lesson; reviewing the process with students; modeling thinking as necessary; and providing criteria to guide the level of thinking that is expected, assess performance, and help students understand how they can improve their performance.

This type of assessment does not just measure achievement; it provides insight into student creativity and innovative thinking. Simply including creative activities in our lesson plans is not enough. Assessment is needed to promote students' metacognition, or thinking about thinking. When students are able to tell us what strategy they used to help them think of many different ideas, or why they chose the solution they did, they are using metacognition. When students are aware that they are using the creative problem solving and innovation processes, they are applying metacognition.

Valuing Feedback

The purposes of feedback are to motivate students, to enhance their engagement, to build understanding, and to assess learning. These purposes are served by incorporating constructive feedback in our assessments. Feedback encourages improvement when it is formative, frequent, and specific. Wiliam (2011) claimed that feedback doubles the rate of learning, and Hattie's syntheses of research (2009, 2012) identified feedback as "having one of the greatest effects on student learning" (2012, p. 18). It should be noted, however, that sometimes giving grades or assigning scores can negate constructive comments given in feedback. In one study (Butler, 1988, as cited in Wiliam, 2011), students who received comments only (no scores) improved performance on similar tasks later, compared to students who received comments and scores; this latter group ignored the comments and only looked at the scores. The focus on the grade negated the power of the feedback.

Praise can "get in the way of students receiving feedback about the task and their performance" (Skipper & Douglas, 2011, as cited in Hattie, 2012, p. 22). When we give praise along with other feedback information, students sometimes hear only the praise. "Praise is more effective if infrequent, credible, specific and genuine" (Brophy, 1981, as cited in Wiliam, 2011, p. 111). The quality of the praise makes more of a difference than the quantity. It is best to give praise after a task is completed; if it is given during the ongoing process, it can divert attention from the task. Praise is most effective when it relates to specific performance on specific criteria.

Kluger and DeNisi's (1996) meta-analysis of studies addressing effects of different types of feedback suggested that effective feedback answers the questions: "Where am I going?

How am I going? Where to next?" (Hattie, 2009, p. 177). For example, in a 2nd grade class's literacy lesson, the teacher always asks students to come up with many different ways to solve the problem in the story. The students know where they are going: they are being assessed on fluency (how many ideas) and flexibility (how many different kinds of ideas). The teacher provides Harry with feedback that tells him how he is doing: she notes that he came up with five different ideas to solve the problem in a story in September, and 12 different ideas in November, and she stresses to him that this is an indication of improvement in his ability to generate ideas. Her encouragement for him to continue this trend tells Harry where to go next. Her feedback for Anne, who has also increased the number of ideas generated, focuses on increasing the variety among her ideas because her ideas are all similar—specific advice on how Anne can improve her creativity in the area of flexibility. In this case, the teacher acts like a coach, providing tips and encouragement on a specific task.

Timing of feedback is critical. "If feedback is given too quickly, students become dependent upon teachers for answers rather than persevering and figuring out problems on their own" (Bangert-Drowns, Kulik, Kulik, & Morgan, 1991, as cited in Goodwin & Miller, 2012, p. 83). Giving students feedback when they are learning new information helps prevent them from forming misconceptions. After a certain point in the learning process, when students are practicing or applying content information, students should have time to self-assess and self-correct prior to receiving feedback from the teacher. Student self-assessment (particularly in error detection) can enhance their metacognition by focusing their attention on their thinking processes. Students should assess themselves on effort, focus, and their time on task—not only ability. The teacher's role in self-assessment is to coach students by asking them such questions as, "Are there any strategies you tried?" or "How might you have used your time more wisely?"

It does take time to provide students with feedback. However, we do not need to comment on everything that needs to be improved; focusing on two or three main points still helps students. Just making one suggestion for improvement as well as commenting on one student strength is providing effective feedback. Teachers can even create feedback slips to use, with space for one or two areas of strength, three points to be improved, and one suggestion for improvement.

Another way to provide feedback is by conducting three-minute conferences with individual students while other students are engaged in a classroom activity or quiet writing or research. In some cases, teachers provide feedback to students during advisory periods, prep time, or before or after school. Teachers also can meet with small groups of students who need the same type of feedback. In personal conferences, use words to empower students and let them know that they have control over their learning. Students should understand that if they listen to feedback and apply it, then their achievement will improve. Students need to feel they have control over their learning (autonomy) and also need to see how effort pays off. Recognizing the benefits of effort even after failure can help students develop the growth mindset (Dweck, 2006) essential to engagement in learning.

Teachers save time by providing feedback where it counts. Fisher and Frey (2012) recommend fixing *errors* rather than *mistakes*—after all, mistakes are simply mistakes and do not reflect a lack of knowledge. Students can fix mistakes. According to Fisher and Frey, however, errors are different: they affect learning. Fisher and Frey (2012) identified four types of errors:

- *Factual errors,* which reflect a lack of knowledge or understanding.
- *Procedural errors,* which occur when students know and understand the content but cannot apply it.

- *Transformation errors,* when students incorrectly apply content information to a new situation.
- *Misconception errors,* when students form ideas based upon incorrect content information.

When students are thinking creatively, they are applying known or learned content and extending their knowledge by considering possibilities, options, and solutions. If their knowledge is inaccurate or they apply information incorrectly, it does affect their ability to think creatively.

There are a variety of technology tools that teachers can use to enhance the feedback experience, and which also may help streamline the process for teachers. Hattie's research on effective feedback (2012) included the use of computer-assisted instructional feedback specific to goals. Teachers can use technology to generate e-mail messages or feedback documents for students (see "Grab and Go" Idea #38), comment on student work via a wiki or electronic journaling, or use a program such as My Access (Vantage Learning; see www.vantagelearning.com/products/my-access-school-edition) to generate feedback based on set criteria.

Relating Creativity to Content

There is a symbiotic relationship between content and creativity: you cannot be creative unless you have something to be creative about. When assessing student responses, it is important to sort out whether the student is making a mistake or an error. Does the student lack content knowledge? Is the student unable to apply content knowledge? Or does the student need more practice in creative thinking? One way to determine this is to substitute a creative thinking verb for a verb at the knowledge, comprehension, or application level (see Chapter 3's discussion about replacing key verbs with creative thinking verbs).

For example, as part of their study of plate tectonics, students write a scenario based upon the elimination of a condition that usually contributes to the plates shifting. When students do not respond, the teacher asks them to list conditions that contribute to the shifting of the plates. If students are able to respond to the factual question correctly and make a list, then it is the creativity twist to the prompt that is the challenge; students are unable to think flexibly about this situation. They might be unable to imagine the elimination of a condition and the effects of such a situation. We can only coach students effectively when we know why they are having difficulty.

Whether the student is struggling with the creative thinking process or the content itself, scaffolding cues can help them become unstuck; teachers can give clues or partial answers to help students complete their response. Day and Cordon (1993, as cited in Wiliam, 2011) studied a group of 3rd graders, half of whom were given a scaffold response when they were stuck and half a complete solution. Students who received the scaffold response learned more and retained the solution longer than the full-solution group.

Keeping track of students who need help with their creativity skills also enables teachers to determine what type of mistakes students are making. Teachers can use a chart to track which students are having trouble with what skills; the chart should list all areas of creativity the teacher is incorporating (i.e., fluency, flexibility, originality, elaboration, imagination, innovation, and creative problem solving). This type of data can help confirm or refute subjective impressions of students and also help identify patterns—either individually or among groups of students—to guide teacher scaffolding of instruction and differentiation of material.

Identifying Creative Learning Goals

Wiggins (2012, p. 11) described feedback as "information about how we are doing in our efforts to reach a goal." Effective feedback requires that students have a goal, take action to achieve it, and receive goal-related feedback on their progress. If students know what the goal is, than constructive feedback will make sense to them; otherwise "'feedback' is just someone telling them what to do" (Brookhart, 2012, p. 24).

Creative learning goals should be "a statement of what students will know or be able to do" (Marzano, 2009, p. 13), and should target the content, thinking process, and product in the lesson. In presenting goals to students, identify the verb and connect the thinking skill with the content, and then identify the product form. For example, the creative thinking lesson "students will demonstrate understanding of grade-appropriate text by creating an audio, video, or multimedia portrayal; and will critique each other's presentations" is adapted from the Common Core State Standard for English language arts (RI.7.7; NGA Center, 2010a) asking students to compare and contrast formats and analyze media. For this creativity lesson, the teacher will provide feedback on the goals: interpret text, create a product (the audio, video, or multimedia version), and critique other products. This gives the original standard a bit of a creativity boost: students still need to do an analysis of the text, but they can create an original product that allows them to show what they know in their own way. The rubric for the assignment includes guidelines for assessing the student's ability to create a portrayal of the text information that is unusual or unique in some way.

When the verb changes, the focus of the goal changes. Figure 7.1 illustrates how to rework goals based on academic standards to incorporate higher-level learning and creativity.

FIGURE 7.1

Creative Learning Goals

Standard	Goal	Adapted Standard	Goal
Compare and contrast a text to an audio, video, or multimedia version of the text, analyzing each medium's portrayal of the subject (e.g., how the delivery of a speech affects the impact of the words). (RI.7.7)	Content: text and media construct; subject portrayal	Create an audio, video, or multimedia version portrayal of the subject of a grade-appropriate text.	Content: text and media construct; subject portrayal
	Thinking process: compare and contrast; analyze		Thinking process: create; analyze
	Product: report		Product: choice of medium
Solve word problems involving addition and subtraction of fractions referring to the same whole and having like denominators, e.g., by using visual fraction models and equations to represent the problem. (4.NF.B.3d)	Content: add/subtract fractions with like denominators; fraction models and equations	Create word problems involving addition and subtraction of fractions having like denominators, e.g., by using visual fraction models and equations to represent the problem.	Content: add/subtract fractions with like denominators; fraction models and equations
	Thinking process: solve		Thinking process: create
	Product: worksheet		Product: word problems

Note. CCSS = Common Core State Standards (National Governors Association Center for Best Practices, Council of Chief State School Officers, 2010a, 2010b).

Learning goals are anchored in standards; they are the foundation for everything we expect students to know and be able to do. Students need to be aware of their creative learning goals so that they know what skill they are supposed to be learning and how they will be assessed. The way we specify creative learning goals is by talking about them with students and by including them in our assignment rubrics.

Some teachers struggle with using a rubric to guide student learning while also differentiating instruction for students based on ability, interest, learning profile (Tomlinson, 1999), and cognitive style (see discussion in Chapter 1). In order to determine if struggling students meet their learning goals, teachers may differentiate their assessment. Teachers can require students to answer fewer questions, write shorter answers, or record their answers. If students participate in the same lesson and respond to the same prompt, they can use the same rubric (Southern Maine Partnership, 2005)—even if they read different material or create a modified product. When developing rubrics for creative learning goals, bear in mind that the thinking process and the skill (in addition to the content and the product) are the focus.

Applying Assessment Tools

Although teachers are often uncomfortable assessing creative thinking because they feel it is too subjective, there are assessment tools that minimize subjectivity while providing students with effective feedback. Criterion-referenced tests of creativity, such as the test designed for use with the Talents Unlimited Thinking Skills Model (see Mobile County Public Schools, 1974), provide a score for fluency, flexibility, and originality. Standardized divergent thinking tests (e.g., the Torrance tests; Torrance, 1987b) also are designed to assess creativity in isolation; that is, they are not tied to content. They can be helpful in assessing students' fluency, flexibility, originality, and elaboration.

However, most teachers are not interested in administering either a creativity standardized test or a criterion-referenced test—most teachers simply are not interested in giving their students more tests. What they want, and are willing to use, is an assessment instrument that is easy to use, provides effective feedback, and takes minimal time to create.

Mini Rubric Strips and Rubrics

The good news is that the rubrics we already use can easily be adapted to also assess creativity. Our rubrics already specify the content and the product of the lesson; teachers only need to add, in effect, one or more rows to their existing rubric to address the thinking skill. Teachers can use a mini rubric strip to assess creative thinking skills or a creative thinking process. Figure 7.2 provides an example of mini rubric strips; each row addresses each of the four creative thinking skills (i.e., fluency, flexibility, originality, elaboration) plus the two processes (innovation and creative problem solving).

When we adapt or rework our lesson plans to incorporate creative thinking skills and processes, as described in the preceding chapters, we also need to adapt or rework the rubric to incorporate these elements. Figure 3.3 illustrated how to target creativity within a standards-based lesson. Figure 7.3 provides sample rubric language for each of the creative thinking skills targeted in the sample 3rd grade literacy lesson based on *Sarah, Plain and Tall* (MacLachlan, 1985). You will notice that the language is a bit different from the mini rubric strip language; this is necessary to make the assessment relevant to the goals of the specific lesson. Feel free to use the mini rubric assessment strips in isolation when just focusing on the thinking skill, embed them by modifying the descriptors to match the content of the lesson, or use the mini rubric strip to help you create a new complete rubric for a lesson.

In creating rubrics for creative thinking learning goals, the teacher must make it clear whether, for example, fluency (i.e., generating many ideas) is the only important criterion or if the quality of the responses will be considered as well. As students become more adept at creative thinking, the quality of the responses, quantity and quality of evidence, innovation, and ability to present reasoning can all be rolled into the same rubric.

It is important to use the shared vocabulary surrounding creativity in the rubric. This means including creative thinking

FIGURE 7.2

Mini Rubric Strips:
Assessing Creative Thinking and Processes

Creative Thinking Skill or Process	1 Not So Great	2 OK	3 Good	4 Great!
Fluency	One or no appropriate ideas	Few appropriate ideas	Some appropriate ideas	Many appropriate ideas
Flexibility	One or two different kinds of ideas or changes	Few different ideas or changes	Some different ideas or changes	Many different ideas or changes
Originality	Used other people's ideas	Few original ideas	Some original ideas	Highly unique and/or unusual idea(s)
Elaboration	Very little description	Some details that support the facts	Details include descriptive language and enable depth of understanding	Highly elaborative; really paints a picture
Innovation	Has difficulty planning and organizing an ordinary idea; is unable to execute it	Uses a framework to plan and organize a somewhat innovative idea; is able to produce it	Uses a framework to plan and organize an innovative idea that is novel and appropriate; is able to produce it	Uses a framework to plan and organize an innovative idea that is novel, appropriate, more effective, and has value; is able to produce it
Creative problem solving process	Doesn't apply problem solving process	Uses problem solving process with faulty and/or ineffective thinking	Uses problem solving process inclusive of critical and creative thinking	Uses problem solving process to produce sophisticated, unusual solutions

FIGURE 7.3

Sample Rubric for Standards-Based Activity Targeting Creative Thinking Skills

(*Sarah, Plain and Tall*; MacLachlan, 1985)

Creative Thinking Skill	Not So Hot	OK	Well Done	Goes Beyond
Fluency Small groups of students brainstorm and list all the situations in Sarah's life that prepared her for being a mother. They provide references to the text to support their ideas and create a graphic organizer.	0 or only 1 situation listed; is not relevant or is illogical	2–3 situations listed are logical, but not very relevant	4–5 situations listed are logical and relevant	6 or more ideas; some situations demonstrate unusual, logical ideas
Flexibility Small groups of students discuss and list how the story would be different if Sarah were a mean mother. They provide references to the text where changes would occur in the storyline and how these would affect the overall story arc.	0 or only 1 effect listed; no demonstration of cause and effect thinking	2–3 effects listed; one different type of effect; mostly demonstrate cause and effect thinking	4–5 effects listed; few different types of effects; all demonstrate logical, cause and effect thinking	6 or more effects listed; many different types of effects; some demonstrate unusual, logical ideas and effects
Originality Small groups of students develop a contextually appropriate, unique process for finding a wife other than advertising. They provide references to the text where changes to the storyline would occur and discuss how these would affect the overall story arc.	1–2 ideas, one of which may not fit contextually	3–4 ideas that are common and fit contextually	5 ideas, one of which stands out above the rest and all of which fit contextually	6 or more ideas, 2 of which are unusual or unique and all of which fit contextually
Elaboration Sarah was never married before and had no children of her own; in their groups, students discuss why taking on someone else's children could have been a challenge for her and develop written products distilling their ideas. They provide references to the text to support their ideas.	0 or only 1 challenge listed that is not relevant or is illogical; no elaboration in their written summary	2–3 challenges listed are logical but not very relevant; details included in 1 or 2 challenges in their written summary	4–5 challenges listed are logical and relevant; details included in 3 or 4 challenges in their written summary are quite vivid and add to the reader's depth of understanding	6 or more challenges listed demonstrate unusual ideas that are logical and relevant, and details in their written summary are highly expressive and make an impact

verbs such as *generate, connect, relate, design, create, produce, construct, elaborate, embellish, predict, improve,* and *substitute*—verbs that connote the creative process. (See Chapter 3 for more about using creative thinking verbs.)

There is no set order for addressing creative thinking skills, so some rubrics will build from fluent to flexible to original thinking, and some will jump from fluent to original thinking without addressing flexible thinking. In any case, the rubric should clearly indicate the targets. Rubrics also should always remind students that there are some limits: all of their creative ideas must make sense contextually, logically, rationally; be relevant and content based; and reflect depth of understanding.

In lessons where students are expected to use their imagination along with creative thinking skills, the rubric needs to reflect how well students used their imagination. Figure 4.4 provided an example of a rubric that reflects content-based creative thinking skills combined with imagination. Notice in that rubric that details are listed as a way to address imagination. Teachers can add a separate imagination criterion if they choose, while also providing students with specific feedback on their use of fluency, flexibility, originality, and elaboration. Such a criterion might reflect ideas or details that are imaginative, unordinary, symbolic, reflective, inspirational, fanciful, enterprising, visionary and/or idealistic.

Rubrics designed for lessons targeting innovation must reflect the involvement of multiple creative thinking areas (see Figure 5.5). In addition to generating multiple ideas, students developing innovative ideas should pay attention to quality and uniqueness as well as to the process itself—and often to the product (Creativity Road 4), too. For example, one 3rd grade class is reading *Sarah, Plain and Tall* (MacLachlan, 1985); the teacher has decided to use a standards-based prompt targeting innovative thinking (see Figure 5.3). To help her students explore the text and think deeply about it, she has asked them to "identify a need in the story that a character has and create an innovative tool to address the need." Figure 7.4 provides the rubric she will use to assess students' performance for this activity (and which, as previously discussed, provides students with guidance for their work).

FIGURE 7.4

Sample Rubric for Lesson Targeting Creativity and Innovation

Lesson Elements*	Not So Hot	OK	Well Done	Goes Beyond
Identify needs via text references	1–2 obvious needs; text reference OK	3–4 common needs; text reference OK	5 needs, some common and some less obvious; text references OK	6 or more needs, some common and at least 1 or 2 unique or very unusual; text references OK
Innovative process	Skips steps or steps are unclear; no evidence of creative thinking	Steps basically described; evidence of minimal creative thinking	Steps described completely; evidence of some creative thinking	Steps described in detail; evidence of in-depth creative thinking
Innovative tool	Construction falls apart; purpose is unclear	Construction holds together but is messy; purpose is obvious but common	Construction is solid and design is simple; purpose is innovative	Construction is sophisticated and detailed; purpose is complex and highly innovative

*See Figure 5.3.

In developing rubrics for lessons targeting innovation, teachers can identify each step of the process as its own criterion and assess specifically how students perform each step. If teachers feel the students do well with the overall process, then there may be no need to break down the steps. Feedback should include how well students thought of many different kinds of ideas and how well they applied criteria to choose their best idea. In lessons targeting innovation, students are assessed on their ability to conceptualize their best idea and their plan to carry it out. Students need to use "what if" thinking when developing and testing their idea, anticipating potential problems. Students are assessed on their ability to reflect on this process as well as the actual product, innovative design. Teachers can incorporate specific criteria when they find out what students plan to do for a product, or retain generic criteria and performance indicators that will work with a variety of products (see Figure 7.5).

FIGURE 7.5

Sample Rubric for Innovative Process

Process and Product	Not So Hot	OK	Well Done	Goes Beyond
5-step description	5 steps, incomplete	5 complete steps; basic responses; some critical and creative thinking	5 complete steps; detailed responses; evidence of critical and creative thinking	5 complete steps; detailed responses demonstrate insight; evidence of in-depth critical and creative thinking
Innovative design	No innovation	Minimal detail; attempt at an innovation but does not work well	Some detail; appears innovative	Very detailed; clearly innovative

In Chapter 5, I discussed a lesson that included both group and individual work. In this type of lesson, students self-assess on how well their *group* uses the innovative process. If a group is not having success generating ideas, the teacher should brainstorm ideas with them, encouraging students to use what they know to come up with seemingly crazy and far-out ideas. It can help to remind students that sometimes a far-out idea might spark a more realistic idea; this type of brainstorming also helps to loosen up their thinking so they can evaluate their ideas and begin to focus on what might be the best choice.

Quality Rating Scale

The quality rating scale (QRS; Curry & Samara, 1999; Drapeau, 2009) provides an alternative to using a rubric when assessing students' creativity. The QRS breaks down the steps in the thinking process and describes the levels of performance within each step. The QRS can assess only the thinking process or include the content and the product of a lesson as well. The QRS can be used with specific students who need more guidance, or it can be used with the whole class.

Unlike a rubric, there is no language in the QRS that describes anything less than top quality. There is no progression of performance to show students how to move from one level of performance to another, only the quality goal. A rubric, in a way, offers students the choice to perform at a lower level than expectation; some students will decide that a 3 on the rubric is good enough. In contrast, the QRS is more straightforward and describes only what is expected.

The teacher, student, or both rate the student's performance on each component on the quality rating scale from 1 to 5. If students score low in a particular area, there is space for them to indicate what they plan to do next time to bring the score up to top quality. If all their scores are high, students are still expected to choose one area that they want to focus on for next time. (Teachers also need to monitor whether students are rating themselves accurately.) If all the criteria are not of equal weight, the teacher can specify how many points each criterion is worth in the overall assignment.

The QRS is designed to give students feedback and guide them in developing quality creative ideas. The criteria and the quality response descriptors reflect both the targeted creative thinking skill and the content of the lesson. In developing a QRS, it is important to include the shared language surrounding creativity so that students understand the expectations and criteria for their performance.

For example, in a 4th grade math unit, the teacher asked students to think of many and unusual ways decimals are used in real life (4.NF.C.6; NGA Center 2010b); the idea was to extend their thinking about how decimals are used. The teacher stressed the word *many* to let students know that fluency was their targeted creative thinking skill, and went on to specify that she was looking for *at least six* creative responses. One student listed radio station designation, weight, mileage, e-mail addresses, website addresses, linear measurement, and math problems. On the QRS (see Figure 7.6), the student received a 5 for fluency, even though not all of her responses represented a numerical decimal relationship. She received a 3 for accuracy because two of her answers (i.e., e-mail addresses and website addresses) were incorrect, and a 4 for unusual ideas because few students thought of the radio station designation. Because her lowest score was on the accuracy criterion, this was the area she focused on for improvement.

The beauty of the QRS is that it has a specific focus, allowing teacher and students to identify strengths and weaknesses. This knowledge helps the student understand what to do next time to improve performance, and helps the teacher consider what kind of scaffolding might be needed to provide students with the help they need.

The QRS may include components such as independence and time on task; these types of self-regulatory behaviors can be part of either a class QRS or an individual student's. For example, in a 6th grade science unit students are exploring levers and pulleys; within this lesson, the teacher wants to target creative thinking and independence. The teacher asks students to make up an *original and unique* conversation between a lever and a pulley; students will be scored on the information that is presented in the dialogue and the way the information is presented. One student (see Figure 7.7) gives herself a 3 on dialogue content because even though her information is accurate and makes a point, the dialogue is not particularly humorous or unique in any way. In fact, the student calls her own writing piece "boring." This self-awareness that she needs help in moving from simply reporting information to descriptive writing suggests to the teacher that, next time, she might be supported with specific elaboration strategies such as the ones described in Chapter 2. The student gives herself a 5 in dialogue skills and independence because she knows dialogue skills and she is a capable student who stays focused on her work.

FIGURE 7.6

Sample Quality Rating Scale with Student Response: Fluency

Elements	Quality	Rating (1–5)	Next Time ...
Content: Reflects knowledge of decimals	Ideas are accurate Ideas are logical Ideas relate to the prompt	3	*I need to slow down and think more carefully about the content.* *I need to review my answers to make sure they are correct.*
Thinking process: Fluency, many ideas	More than 6 ideas	5	
Thinking process: Unusual ideas	Ideas are uncommon	4	
Product: List	Readable	5	

FIGURE 7.7

Sample Quality Rating Scale with Student Response: Originality

Elements	Quality	Rating (1–5)	Next Time ...
Content: Dialogue information	Makes sense Conveys content information Makes a point Information is accurate	5	
Thinking process: Original and unique	Expression is unique Demonstrates humor	3	*My dialogue sounds boring and does not stand out as unique.*
Product: Dialogue skills	Dialogue is correctly written Spelling is accurate Grammar is accurate Long enough to engage the reader	5	
Independence	Works on own Focused during work time	5	

Imagination is difficult to assess, but the degree to which a student applies a particular strategy to access imagination can be rated. When assessing a lesson focusing on imagination, use the shared vocabulary and stress the importance of detail in the final product. A strategy that is commonly used with imagination is visualization. In a middle school lesson, students were studying the Minoans. The teacher asked the students to close their eyes and imagine a society where men and women treat each other with equal respect. She asked them to visualize these people's clothes, expressions, activities, and so on. When students opened their eyes, she asked them to describe what they saw, heard, and smelled in their visualization, and to write their description in a three-paragraph essay. After the students completed the assignment, they filled out a QRS. One student gave himself a 3 in the content area; he did not feel he knew enough about the Minoans to build a strong visualization. His descriptions were scored similarly—he was unable to add imagery, and his product lacked detail. It is difficult to imagine that which you know little about. Creativity begins with knowledge.

When using a QRS with innovation or the creative problem solving process, the rating scale reflects the process, and each step in the process may be scored. For example, a QRS for a lesson in which students are using the creative problem solving process might include the following:

- *Identify problems*—teacher indicates how many is "many," that problems must be solvable and make sense contextually or conceptually, and that problems may be both literal and inferred.
- *Choose a problem*—students must identify which problem is the overarching problem or the most significant.
- *Identify solutions*—students must identify many solutions, both real and imaginary.
- *Choose a solution*—the solution must solve the problem, have the greatest impact, and be realistic contextually or conceptually.
- *Create a plan*—plan is specific and provides step-by-step implementation.

Creative thinking lessons often include creative products (Creativity Road 4), which can be oral, written, visual, kinesthetic, or technology based. Figure 7.8 lists different types of creative products. A QRS can be used to assess creative products, too; in this case, it would describe requirements for the product and assess how the student applies creativity in the actual product

FIGURE 7.8

Creative Products

Oral	Written	Visual	Kinesthetic	Technology Based
Speech/presentation	Critique	Cartoon	Flip-card games	Electronic game
Dialogue	Summary	Time line	Charades/movement game	Electronic field trip
Lesson	Script	Graphic organizer	Collage	Crossword puzzle
Song or rap	Reworked ending	Poster	Demonstration	Shared writing/ collaborative storytelling
Newscast/TV commentary	Report/essay	Outline	Museum exhibit/display	Character scrapbook
Choral speaking	Story problem	Book jacket/brochure	Experiment	Electronic binder
Discussion	Diary	Checklist	Board game	Fake Facebook page
Interview/Q&A	Letter	Design/drawing	Puppet show	Slideshow presentation
Debate	Journal	Flowchart	Invention	Blog
Explanation	Short story	Illustration	Mobile	Animation
Oral report	Tall tale/myth	Advertisement	Skit/play/role-play	Interactive time line
Storytelling	Editorial	Bumper sticker	Game show	Graph
Joke	Poem	Photo essay	Model	Web/multimedia poster
	Questionnaire	Labeled picture	Scavenger hunt	Graphic novel
	Scenario	Slideshow	Relief rubbing	Word collage/cloud
		Map	3D pop-up book	
		Mural	Museum box	
		Painting		
		Trading cards		

form. For example, if the teacher asks students to create lyrics for a known melody, then the QRS criteria would focus on how creative and meaningful the lyrics are. Creativity can be assessed in such a project by how well the lyrics fit the melody and clever play with the words.

Visual products, on the other hand, sometimes require minimal to no writing—although they still require the student to understand the content. Visual products are a good way to support, encourage, and recognize ability in students who struggle with writing, are English-language learners, or simply prefer the visual arts to other subjects. A visual product QRS would require students to meet format, content, and creativity criteria such as visual appeal, appropriate and relevant quotes or images, and unique interpretation of text or application of a concept.

In the 21st century classroom, the four traditional product modality types do not meet the needs of students who are technology focused and who prefer to use technology-based products to demonstrate what they know. Most students have access to computers at home or know where to go to access computers after school. Most students are very familiar with a variety of technologies; in the creative classroom, then, our goal should be to introduce them to new types of technology products or provide assignments using technology-based programs. The QRS can easily be adapted to these types of lessons. For example, if students are creating a digital story, their QRS might include to what degree their message/story makes sense (content), how many visuals they used to convey their message/story (thinking process: fluency), how unique their message/story is (thinking process: originality), and how visually pleasing and organized their images are (product).

Defining Grades

Grades do not help students to improve their performance; feedback does. "When we give a grade as part of our feedback, students routinely read only as far as the grade" (Johnson, 2012, p. 64). Many teachers prefer to use rubrics and rating scales, especially once they have compiled a bank of ready-made templates. However, most teachers still need to generate overall performance grades according to the requirements of their district or state. Teachers can convert the descriptors on rubrics and mini rubrics into grades. For example, "Goes beyond" equals an *A*, "Well done" equals a *B*, "OK" equals a *C*, and "Not so hot" is a *D* or *F*. However, because each criterion varies in importance, a "Well done" or *B* in an accurate content criterion does not have the same value as a "Well done" or *B* in fluency. In this case, teachers would need to weight individual criteria before arriving at a total score. The QRS also can be converted to grades. When using the QRS, a student who receives all 5s on the rating scale receives an *A*, a 4 equals a *B*, 3 is a *C*, 2 is a *D*, and 1 is failing. Again, not all of the criteria are of equal worth. It is essential that students (and their families) understand the difference between feedback and grading and how grading is done in the creative classroom.

Self-Assessment

Feedback is only as effective as the learning that results from it. If students do not take action on the feedback, then there will be no improvement. This is also true of student self-reflection: if students learn from self-assessment and take action, then it is well worth the time spent.

Students can score their own rubric, mini rubric, or QRS. If teachers provide exemplars that describe what a "5" is or what "goes beyond" looks like, then students have a model to follow. Teachers and students can conduct a shared review, where students score themselves and the teacher also scores them on the same assignment. The student compares the scores and meets with the teacher if there are questions or if the student disagrees with the teacher's scores.

In one 4th grade class, the teacher developed a creative thinking literacy unit on the text *Because of Winn-Dixie* (DiCamillo, 2000). The standard addressed was "Describe in depth a character, setting, or event in a story or drama, drawing on specific details in the text (e.g., a character's thoughts, words, or actions)" (RL.4.3; NGA Center, 2010a). The assignment was for students first to list all the various words that describe Opal in the book and cite details from the book. Next, students brainstormed a list of many different adjectives to describe an imaginary friend whom Opal could have had. Then students wrote a story summary integrating the imaginary friend while minimally impacting the storyline. This creative thinking exercise required thorough content knowledge while also promoting all four creative thinking skills. Upon completion of the assignment, the teacher used both student self-assessment and a shared review:

- Students completed a self-monitoring review assessing their level of performance surrounding the content, thinking process, and product, citing reasons for the individual scores (see sample, Figure 7.9).
- The teacher and individual students completed a shared review, a collaborative tool providing an overview of the students' performance in all areas of the activity, both content related and creativity related (see sample, Figure 7.10).

The three "grab and go" ideas at the end of this chapter include a teacher tool, a combination teacher/student tool, and a student self-reflection form. For students to be able to effectively self-assess, they need to be able to distinguish between errors and mistakes. As mentioned previously, mistakes do not reflect a lack of knowledge and can be fixed; errors, however, affect learning and need to be addressed (Fisher & Frey, 2012). The self-assessment process promotes metacognition by requiring students to examine their thinking processes; this is an area teachers and students may want to monitor for progress over time. This reflective process has students consider in what areas they demonstrate creativity, whether they can describe their creative thinking processes, and how well they use creative thinking. Like other self-assessments, students must be ready to provide evidence for their responses.

FIGURE 7.9

Sample Student Self-Assessment

Assignment: List many varied words to describe Opal in *Because of Winn-Dixie*. Brainstorm many different words to describe her imaginary friend. Integrate the imaginary friend into the story without impacting the original story. Write a summary of *Because of Winn-Dixie* adding an imaginary friend for Opal.

Assignment Element	Oops! Missed It	I Did This a Bit	I Did What Was Expected	I Did Great With This!
Standard: What's your evidence?			*I cited text evidence.*	
Content: What's your evidence you understood the content?			*I wrote words to describe Opal. I retold the story.*	
Creative thinking process: What's your evidence you used creative thinking?				*I came up with many different words to describe Opal's imaginary friend.*
Product: What's your evidence the product met all the requirements?				*My story summary had the imaginary friend in it, made sense, was organized, had no run-on sentences, and was interesting.*

FIGURE 7.10

Sample Shared Review

Student name: Sally Sawyer	Date: December 12, 2013
Assignment: List many varied words to describe Opal in *Because of Winn-Dixie*. Brainstorm many different words to describe her imaginary friend. Integrate the imaginary friend into the story without impacting the original story. Write a summary of *Because of Winn-Dixie* adding an imaginary friend for Opal.	
Student's review	
When addressing the goals of the lesson, my strengths are …	I brainstormed many adjectives to describe Opal and Opal's imaginary friend. I wrote a good summary.
While addressing the goals of the lesson, I learned …	I learned to pay attention to the adjectives. I also learned to think about how characters have reasons why they act the way they do.
My favorite part of the lesson was …	My favorite part of the lesson was creating an imaginary friend for Opal. I had to think about what kind of friend she would like to have.
Next time, I need to work on …	I need to work on thinking of words that aren't in the story but go along with the action in the story.
Teacher's comments	
When addressing the goals of the lesson, I believe your strengths are … *Brainstorming — I agree with you! You are a very good brainstormer; you often come up with many interesting words.*	
When addressing the goals of the lesson, I believe next time you might focus on … *I agree you should think really hard about what you read so you can come up with inferential ideas about your reading, not just the words that are literally on the page.* *I also think you might watch how you structure your paragraphs. For example, in the second paragraph, the third sentence is on a different topic, so it should be in a different paragraph. Remember to have one main idea in each paragraph.*	

Reflecting on and Extending Chapter Information

1. In what ways might effective feedback on creative thinking improve learning?
2. Of all the assessment tools mentioned in this chapter, which is the one you are most likely to use and why?
3. How can you use feedback and assessment to increase student motivation and engagement?
4. Why does goal setting play a significant role in the assessment process?
5. How can you help parents understand the importance of feedback as compared to grades?

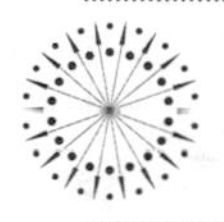

"Grab and Go" Idea #38

Feedback Form

Teachers can use technology to help streamline their feedback process. A template such as Figure 7.11's sample can be maintained as a Word document and adapted to add additional criteria specific to individual assignments. The teacher creates a bank of descriptors that can be plugged in and used over and over again for different students. Continue to brainstorm descriptors; then just cut and paste to create personalized feedback.

FIGURE 7.11

Feedback Template
The goals for this assignment were:
You did very well in the following areas:
I see you had some problems in some areas:
Next time, I would like you to focus on:
Here are a few comments on your self-regulatory skills: Time on task: Level of independence: Effort:

"Grab and Go" Idea #39

Hunt for ME (Mistakes and Errors)

This tool is designed to support both teacher and student. The teacher reviews student work and lists the number of mistakes and errors the student made. Then the student reviews the work, hunts for the same mistakes and errors and identifies them, and corrects the mistakes and errors. If the student is unable to correct the error, this lets the teacher know where to focus instruction or support.

For example (see Figure 7.12), a 7th grade math standard is for students to be able to "use facts about supplementary, complementary, vertical, and adjacent angles in a multi-step problem to write and solve simple equations for an unknown angle in a figure" (7.G.B.5; NGA Center, 2010b). The teacher has designed a lesson plan that requires solving a series of real-life problems, which involve angle measure, area, surface area, and volume. The teacher provides students with eight math problems, and they have to come up with two additional problems on their own. In

FIGURE 7.12

Hunt for ME Form	
Assignment: 10 math problems using angle measure, area, surface area, and volume	Mistakes: 3 Errors: 1
Hunt for ME!	
Mistake: Problem computing area	*multiplication mistake*
Mistake: Problem computing surface area	*multiplication mistake*
Mistake: Problem computing volume	*missed multiplying in a dimension*
Error	*skipped step in a multiple-step word problem*

this example, out of the 10 problems, the student made three mistakes based on computation and one error (solving the whole problem incorrectly). The student has identified all the mistakes and was able to specify the error.

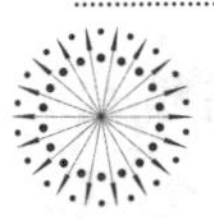

"Grab and Go" Idea #40

Creativity Self-Reporting Form

This reflective process has students consider in what areas they demonstrate creativity, whether they can describe their creative thinking processes, and how well they use creative thinking (see Figure 7.13). Like other self-assessments, students must be ready to provide evidence for their responses.

What would this self-reporting form look like if you completed it?

FIGURE 7.13

Creativity Self-Reporting Form			
My creativity	**Not Really**	**Somewhat**	**Definitely!**
I can talk about my creativity in a lesson.			
I can point out which parts of the lesson I could have responded to more creatively.			
I can suggest ways to improve my creativity.			
I can explain my understanding of creativity and how it affects my responses.			
I can talk about similarities and differences between my creative responses in a lesson and my other responses.			
I can use different creativity techniques to affect my responses.			
If I cannot think of any creative ideas, I know how to help myself become unstuck.			
I can use creativity wisely. I know when and where creativity is appropriate.			
I know when it is more effective to work with a group on something creative.			
I use creativity to help me build deeper understanding of information.			

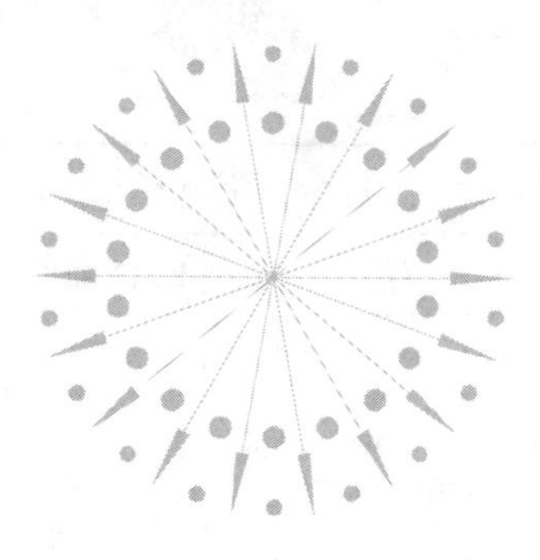

Epilogue

Creativity in the classroom can make a difference when it is intentionally orchestrated. Teachers display posters as visual reminders that creativity is alive and well in their classroom. They post student responses that demonstrate creative thinking and exhibit creative products. They create an accepting classroom climate where calculated risk taking is encouraged and varied ideas are welcome.

Teachers make sure creative activities and lessons happen regularly in their classroom. Students use language specific to creativity. Teachers align creative thinking activities with their curricular standards. The lessons drive student understanding and application of content knowledge. Creative thinking activities are not used to fill time before the end of class or used as a reward for good behavior; they are meaningful and purposeful lessons.

Teachers know that a steady diet of critical thinking lessons denies students the opportunity to engage in "what if" thinking. Teachers attend to different cognitive preferences when they differentiate lessons for students who prefer to think outside the box. Creativity increases motivation and engagement, which often results in an increase in achievement.

In this book, I have presented different tools and strategies to help teachers adapt a lesson, create a lesson, or design a task that promotes creative thinking and creative products. Creativity Road 1 reminds us of the creativity verbs, prompts, and phrases that can easily be used. Creativity Road 2 leads us to strategies that promote creative thinking. Creativity Road 3 defines procedural language for innovative and creative problem solving processes, and Creativity Road 4 points to the use of creative products. When embarking on any of the creativity roads, students deserve feedback on the content, thinking process, and product. There are many feedback tools that provide teachers with ways to make their feedback timely, specific, and effective.

I hope I accomplished my goals in writing this book, which were to help you reach more of your learners, provide you with creativity strategies and tools, and show you how to intentionally use creativity in your classroom. It is not that hard, and the payoff can be great. My final tips include the following:

- Think of yourself as a creative person; eventually you will believe it.
- Do not let the blocks get in your way; they can be overcome.
- Creativity is contagious; surround yourself with creative people.

And most important: Experience the joy of creativity… *every day*.

References

Ali, M. (2011, May 12). *Traditional teaching* [Video file]. Retrieved from http://www.youtube.com/watch?v=-7gLgJQ1auY

Amabile, T. M. (1989). *Growing up creative.* New York: Crown.

Amabile, T. M. (1998, September–October). How to kill creativity. *Harvard Business Review,* 76–87.

Amabile, T. M., Conti, R., Coon, H., Lazenby, J., & Herron, M. (1996). Assessing the work environment for creativity. *Academy of Management Journal, 39,* 1154–1184. http://dx.doi.org/10.2307/256995

Anderson, L., Krathwohl, D. R., Airasian, P. W., Cruikshank, K. A., Mayer, R. E., Pintrich, P. R., & Wittrock, M. C. (2000). *A taxonomy for learning, teaching, and assessing. A revision of Bloom's taxonomy of educational objectives.* Upper Saddle River, NJ: Pearson.

Azzam, A. (2009). Why creativity now? A conversation with Sir Ken Robinson. *Educational Leadership, 67*(1), 22–26. Retrieved from http://www.ascd.org/publications/educational-leadership/sept09/vol67/num01/Why-Creativity-Now¢-A-Conversation-with-Sir-Ken-Robinson.aspx

Baldwin, H. (2012, July 24). Time off to innovate: Good idea or a waste of tech talent? *Computer World* [Online]. Retrieved from http://www

.computerworld.com/s/article/9229373/Time_off_to_innovate_Good_idea_or_a_waste_of_tech_talent_

Barrett, J., & Barrett, R. (1978). *Cloudy with a chance of meatballs.* New York, Simon & Schuster.

Beghetto, R. A. (2005). Does assessment kill student creativity? *The Educational Forum, 69*(3), 254–263. Available: http://dx.doi.org/10.1080/00131720508984694

Beghetto, R. A., & Kaufman, J. C. (Eds.). (2010). *Nurturing creativity in the classroom* [E-reader version]. Cambridge, UK: Cambridge University Press.

Beghetto, R. A., & Kaufman, J. C. (2013). Fundamentals of creativity. *Educational Leadership, 70*(5), 10–15.

Boykin, A. W., & Noguera, P. (2011). *Creating the opportunity to learn: Moving from research to practice to close the achievement gap.* Alexandria, VA: ASCD.

Boykin, A. W., & Noguera, P. (2012, March). Increase in student achievement. *Education Update.* Alexandria, VA: ASCD.

Bridgeland, J. M., Dilulio, J. J., Jr., & Burke Morrison, K. (2006, March). *The silent epidemic: Perspectives of high school dropouts.* Washington, DC: Civic Enterprises. Retrieved from https://docs.gatesfoundation.org/Documents/TheSilentEpidemic3-06FINAL.pdf

Bronson, P., & Merryman, A. (2010, July 10). The creativity crisis. *Newsweek.* Retrieved from http://www.newsweek.com/2010/07/10/the-creativity-crisis.html

Brookhart, S. M. (2008). *How to give effective feedback to your students.* Alexandria, VA: ASCD.

Brookhart, S. M. (2012). Preventing feedback fizzle. *Educational Leadership, 70*(1), 24–29.

Cornell University. (2008, March). *Ken Robinson states imagination and creativity come before innovation* [Lecture/presentation]. Retrieved from http://eclips.cornell.edu/themes.do?isCUWA=ac967&-type=&id=500&clipID=12077&tab=TabClipPage

Csikszentmihalyi, M. (1996). *Creativity: Flow and the psychology of discovery and invention.* New York: Harper Perennial.

Deci, E. L. (1995). *Why we do what we do: Understanding self-motivation.* New York, Penguin.

DiCamillo, K. (2000). *Because of Winn-Dixie.* Somerville, MA: Candlewick Press.

DiSalvo, D. (2011). *What makes your brain happy and why you should do the opposite* [E-reader version]. Amherst, NY: Prometheus.

Drapeau, P. (2004). *Differentiated instruction: Making it work.* New York: Scholastic.

Drapeau, P. (2009). *Differentiating with graphic organizers: Tools to foster critical and creative thinking.* Thousand Oaks, CA: Corwin.

Drapeau, P. (2011). The creative classroom. *Teachers Matter, 13,* 30.

Dweck, C. (2006). *Mindset: The new psychology of success. How we can learn to fulfill our potential.* New York: Ballantine.

Eberle, R. F. (1971). *SCAMPER: Games for imagination development.* Buffalo, NY: DOK Publishing.

Farrell, M. P. (2001). *Collaborative circles: Friendship dynamics and creative work.* Chicago: The University of Chicago Press.

Fincher, D. (Director), & Sorkin, A. (Writer). (2010). *The social network.* United States: Columbia Pictures.

Fisher, D., & Frey, N. (2008). *Better learning through structured teaching: A framework for the gradual release of responsibility.* Alexandria, VA: ASCD.

Fisher, D., & Frey, N. (2012). Making time for feedback. *Educational Leadership, 70*(1), 42–46.

Gardner, H. (1989). *To open minds.* New York: Basic Books.

Goleman, D., Kaufman, P., & Ray, M. (1992). *The creative spirit. Companion to the PBS television series.* New York: Penguin.

Goodwin, B., & Miller, K. (2012). Research says good feedback is targeted, specific, timely. *Educational Leadership, 70*(1), 82–83.

Gordon, W. J. J. (1961). *Synectics: The development of creative capacity.* New York: Harper & Row.

Govindarajan, V. (2010, August). *Innovation is not creativity* [Blog post]. Retrieved from http://blogs.hbr.org/2010/08/innovation-is-not-creativity/

Grant, A., Grant, G., & Gallate, J. (2012). *Who killed creativity?... And how can we get it back?* New York: Wiley.

Hattie, J. (2009). *Visible learning: A synthesis of over 800 meta-analyses relating to achievement.* London: Routledge.

Hattie, J. (2011). *Visible learning for teachers: Maximizing impact on learning.* London: Routledge.

Hattie, J. (2012). Know thy impact. *Educational Leadership, 70*(1), 18–23.

Herby. (2005, September 1). *Hurricane Katrina: Extreme video* [Video file]. Retrieved from http://www.youtube.com/watch?v=s76Qn7bpCsQ

Higgins S., Hall, E., Baumfield, V., & Moseley, D. (2005). *A meta-analysis of the impact of the implementation of thinking skills approaches on pupils.* London: Institute of Education, University of London. Retrieved from https://eppi.ioe.ac.uk/cms/Default.aspx?tabid=339

Hinton, S. E. (1967). *The outsiders.* New York: Viking Press.

Holzer, M. F. (2007, 2009). *Aesthetic education, inquiry and imagination.* New York: Lincoln Center Institute. Available: http://www.lcinstitute.org

Isaksen, S. G., & Treffinger, D. J. (1985). *Creative problem solving: The basic course*. Buffalo, NY: Bearly.

Jensen, E. (2013). *Engaging students with poverty in mind: Practical strategies for raising achievement*. Alexandria, VA: ASCD.

John-Steiner, V. (2000). *Creative collaboration*. New York: Oxford University Press.

Johnson, D. (2012). Power up! / Electronic feedback. *Educational Leadership, 70*, 84–85.

Johnson, S. (2010). *Where good ideas come from: The natural history of innovation*. New York: Riverhead. Available: http://www.ted.com/talks/steven_johnson_where_good_ideas_come_from.html

Karnes, F. A., & Bean, S. M. (2009). *Methods and materials for teaching the gifted* (3rd ed.). Waco, TX: Prufrock Press.

Kaufman, J. C., & Lan, L. (2012). East-west cultural bias and creativity: We are alike and we are different. *Gifted and Talented International, 27*(1), 115–118. Retrieved from http://www.world-gifted.org/sites/default/files/GTI27(1)August2012.pdf

Kaufman, J., Plucker, J. A., & Baer, J. (2008). *Essentials of creativity assessment*. Hoboken, NJ: Wiley & Sons.

Kim, K. H. (2005). Can only people be creative? *Journal of Secondary Gifted Education, 16*, 57–66.

Kirschner, P. A., Sweller, J., & Clark, R. E. (2006). Why minimal guidance during instruction does not work: An analysis of the failure of constructivist, discovery, problem-based, experiential, and inquiry-based teaching. *Educational Psychologist, 41*, 75–86. Available: http://dx.doi.org/10.1207/s15326985ep4102_1

Kluger, A. N., & DeNisi, A. (1996). The effects of feedback interventions on performance: A historical review, a meta-analysis, and a preliminary feedback intervention theory. *Psychological Bulletin, 119*, 254–284. Available: http://dx.doi.org/10.1037/0033-2909.119.2.254

Kramer, N. (2005). *Shaping Earth's surface: Water*. South Yarra, Australia: Macmillan Education.

Liu, E., & Noppe-Brandon, S. (2009, 2010). *Imagination first: Unlocking the power of possibility*. San Francisco: Jossey-Bass.

Long, P. (2010, Winter). My brain on my mind. *American Scholar, 79*(1). Retrieved from http://www.priscillalong.com/my_brain_on_my_mind_90660.htm

MacLachlan, P. (1985). *Sarah, plain and tall*. New York: Scholastic.

Maine Department of Education. (2013, July 23). *Everything in the building is tied to a learning standard* [Video file]. Retrieved from http://www.youtube.com/watch?v=MMWXh5GtZ4E#t=42

Marzano, R. J. (2009). *Designing and teaching learning goals and objectives*. Bloomington, IN: Marzano Research Laboratory.

McAuliffe, J., & Stoskin, L. (1993). *What color is Saturday? Using analogies to enhance creative thinking in the classroom.* Tucson, AZ: Zephyr Press.

McKim, R. (1980). *Experiences in visual thinking* (2nd ed.). Boston: PWS.

Michelli, N., Holzer, M. F., & Bevan, B. (2011). *Learning to imagine.* (Imagination Conversations). New York: Lincoln Center Institute.

Milora, M. T. (1987). The creative attitude. In D. G. Tuerch (Ed.), *Creativity and liberal learning* (pp. 131–146). Norwood, NJ: Ablex.

Mobile County Public Schools. (1974). *Criterion referenced tests of talents.* Mobile, AL: Author.

Murdock, M. C., & Ganim, R. M. (1993). Creativity and humor: Integration and incongruity. *Journal of Creative Behavior, 27,* 57–70. http://dx.doi.org/10.1002/j.2162-6057.1993.tb01387.x

National Governors Association Center for Best Practices, Council of Chief State School Officers. (2010a). *Common core state standards for English language arts & literacy in history/social studies, science, and technical subjects.* Washington, DC: Author. Retrieved from http://www.corestandards.org/the-standards

National Governors Association Center for Best Practices, Council of Chief State School Officers. (2010b). *Common core state standards for mathematics.* Washington, DC: Author. Retrieved from http://www.corestandards.org/the-standards

NGSS Lead States. (2013). *Next generation science standards: For states, by states.* Washington, DC: National Academies Press.

Niu, W., & Sternberg, R. J. (2002). Contemporary studies on the concept of creativity: The east and the west. *Journal of Creative Behavior, 36,* 269–284. Available: http://dx.doi.org/10.1002/j.2162-6057.2002.tb01069.x

Noller, R. B. (1979). *Scratching the surface of creative problem-solving: A bird's eye-view of CPS.* Buffalo, NY: DOK Publishers.

Noppe-Brandon, S., Deasy, R. J., & Gitter, C. (2011). *Findings of the imagination conversations: The lessons of a two-year national initiative.* New York: Lincoln Center Institute.

Ogle, D. M. (1986). K-W-L: A teaching model that develops active reading of expository text. *Reading Teacher, 39,* 564–570.

Osborn, A. F. (1963). *Applied imagination: Principles and procedures of creative thinking.* New York: Scribner.

Pannels, T. C., & Claxton, A. F. (2008). Happiness, creative ideation, and locus of control. *Creativity Research Journal, 20,* 67–71. Available: http://dx.doi.org/10.1080/10400410701842029

Parnes, S. J. (1992). *Sourcebook for creative problem solving.* Buffalo, NY: Creative Education Foundation.

Pearson, J. (1997). *Jon Pearson's draw power: Active tools for teachers and parents.* Chicago: Author.

Pearson, R. (2010). Getting your act(s) together. *The complete handbook of novel writing: Everything you need to know about creating & selling your work* (pp. 64–70). Ontario: Writer's Digest.

Pearson, R. (2012, November 17). *Getting it write: Where imagination meets creativity*. Presentation at the NAGC 59th Annual Convention, Denver, Colorado.

Piirto, J. (2004). *Understanding creativity.* Scottsdale, AZ: Great Potential Press.

Pink, D. H. (2009). *Drive: The surprising truth about what motivates us* [E-reader version]. New York: Penguin.

Robinson, K. (2007). *Do schools kill creativity?* [Video file]. Retrieved from http://www.youtube.com/watch?v=iG9CE55wbtY

Robinson, K. (2011). *Out of our minds: Learning to be creative* [E-reader version]. Chichester, UK: Capstone.

Root-Bernstein, R., & Root-Bernstein, M. (2001). *Sparks of genius: The 13 thinking tools of the world's most creative people.* Boston: Houghton Mifflin.

Rudowicz, E., & Hui, A. (1997). The creative personality: Hong Kong perspective. *Journal of Social Behavior and Personality, 12,* 139–148.

Rudowicz, E., & Yue, X. D. (2000). Concepts of creativity: Similarities and differences among Hong Kong, Mainland, and Taiwanese Chinese. *Journal of Creative Behavior, 34,* 175–192. Available: http://dx.doi.org/10.1002/j.2162-6057.2000.tb01210.x

Sachar, L. (1998). *Holes.* New York: Random House.

Sandburg, C. (1916). The fog. *Chicago poems* (No. 56). New York: Henry Holt.

Sawyer, K. (2013). *Zig zag: The surprising path to greater creativity.* San Francisco: Jossey-Bass.

Sawyer, R. K. (2003). Creative teaching: Collaborative discussion as disciplined improvisation. *Educational Researcher, 33*(2), 12–20. Available: http://dx.doi.org/10.3102/0013189X033002012

Sawyer, R. K. (2006a). Educating for innovation. *Thinking Skills and Creativity, 1,* 41–48. Retrieved from Available: http://www.academia.edu/946010/Educating_for_innovation

Sawyer, R. K. (2006b). *Explaining creativity: The science of human innovation.* New York: Oxford University Press.

Schlichter, C. (1986). Talents unlimited: An inservice education model for teaching thinking skills. *Gifted Child Quarterly, 30,* 119–123. http://dx.doi.org/10.1177/001698628603000305

Seelig, T. (2012). *inGenius: A crash course on creativity.* New York: HarperOne.

Simonton, D. K. (1999). *Origins of genius: Darwinian perspectives on creativity.* New York: Oxford University Press.

Snyder, W. (2013). Using prediction, performance, and feedback to engage the brain in note taking. *Best Practices for Student Engagement, 8*(7). Retrieved from http://www.ascd.org/ascd-express/vol8/807-snyder.aspx

Southern Maine Partnership. (2005). *Instructional differentiation for student independence.* Gorham, ME: University of Southern Maine.

Sprenger, M. (2010). *Brain-based teaching in the digital age.* Alexandria, VA: ASCD.

Stanford University. (2012, May 19). *Unlocking creativity* [Video file]. Retrieved from http://www.youtube.com/watch?v=p1f7NLMM_G0

Sternberg, R. J. (1985): *Beyond IQ: A triarchic theory of human intelligence.* New York: Cambridge University Press.

Sternberg, R. J. (Ed.). (1999). *Handbook of creativity.* Cambridge, UK: Cambridge University Press.

Sternberg, R. J., & Williams, W. M. (1996). *How to develop student creativity.* Alexandria, VA: ASCD.

Tomlinson, C. A. (1999). *The differentiated classroom: Responding to the needs of all learners.* Alexandria, VA: ASCD.

Torok, G. (n.d.). *Don't ignore the nudges* [Blog post]. Retrieved from http://www.torok.com/articles/creativity/DontIgnoreNudges.html

Torrance, E. P. (1987a). *Teaching for creativity.* In S. G. Isaksen (Ed.), *Frontiers of creativity research: Beyond the basics* (pp. 189–215). Buffalo, NY: Bearly.

Torrance, E. P. (1987b). *Torrance tests of creative thinking.* Bensenville, IL: Scholastic Testing.

Treffinger, D. J. (2008). Preparing creative and critical thinkers. *Educational Leadership, 65.* Retrieved from http://www.ascd.org/publications/educational-leadership/summer08/vol65/num09/Preparing-Creative-and-Critical-Thinkers.aspx

Treffinger, D. J., Isaksen, S. G., & Stead-Dorval, K. B. (2006). *Creative problem solving: An introduction* (4th ed.). Waco, TX: Prufrock Press.

Treffinger, D. J., Schoonover, P., & Selby, E. (2013). *Educating for creativity and innovation.* Waco, TX: Prufrock Press.

University of Houston Education. (2014). *What is digital storytelling?* Retrieved from http://digitalstorytelling.coe.uh.edu/page.cfm?id=27&cid=27

University of Indianapolis Center of Excellence in Leadership of Learning. (2009). *Summary of research on project-based learning.* Retrieved from http://cell.uindy.edu/docs/PBL%20research%20summary.pdf

Wagner, T. (2012). *Creating innovators: The making of young people who will change the world.* New York: Scribner.

Wiggins, G. (2012). Seven keys to effective feedback. *Educational Leadership, 70*(1), 10–16.

Wilhelm, J. D. (2002). *Action strategies for deepening comprehension: Using drama strategies to assist improved reading performance.* New York: Scholastic.

William, D. (2011). *Embedded formative assessment.* Bloomington, IN: Solution Tree.

Willis, J. (2006). *Research-based strategies to ignite student learning: Insights from a neurologist and classroom teacher.* Alexandria, VA: ASCD.

Zike, D. (2000). *Dinah Zike's foldables for grades 1–6: 3-D interactive graphic organizers.* New York: Macmillan/McGraw-Hill.

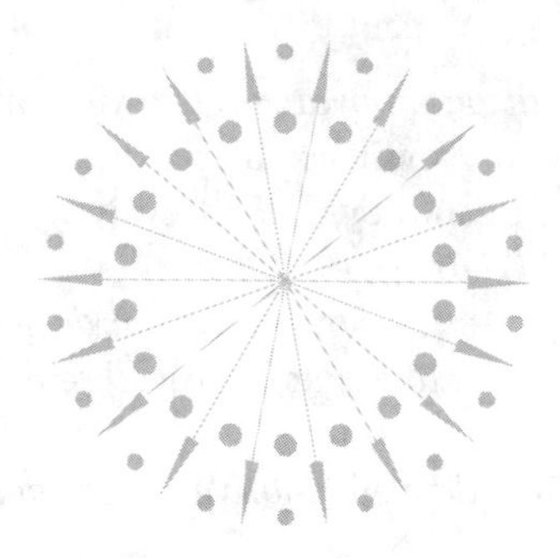

Index

Note: Page locators followed by an italicized *f* indicate information contained in figures.

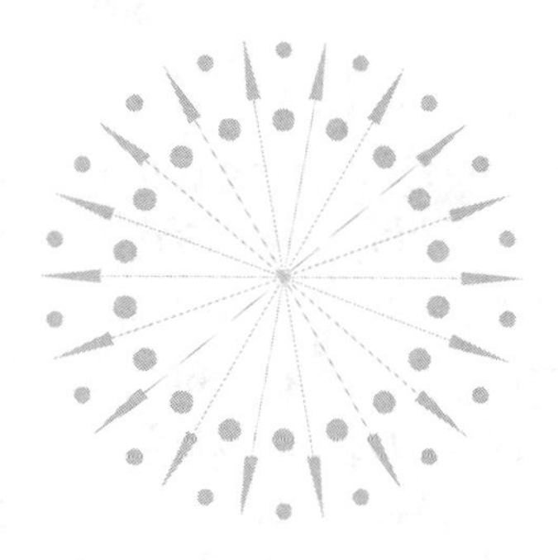

About the Author

Patti Drapeau is an educational consultant, author, and internationally known presenter. Patti has been a keynote presenter at conferences and conducts workshop sessions in school districts in the United States, Canada, Australia, New Zealand, and Singapore. Patti is an adjunct faculty member at the University of Southern Maine and also a consultant for the Maine Department of Education in gifted education. She currently serves on the executive board of the Council of State Directors of Programs for the Gifted.

Patti has over 25 years of classroom experience teaching students of all ages and coordinating programs in Freeport, Maine. Patti received the New England Region Gifted and Talented award for outstanding contributions in gifted education. She also received the Maine Educators of the Gifted and Talented award for exemplary service.

Patti is the author of the books *Great Teaching with Graphic Organizers* (1999); *Differentiated Instruction: Making It Work* (2004); *Differentiating with Graphic Organizers: Tools to Foster Critical and Creative Thinking* (2009); and of the chapter "Graphic Organizers: Tools to Promote Differentiation" in *The Best of Corwin: Differentiated Instruction* (2011). She has written articles for *Understanding Our Gifted* and the New Zealand publication *Teachers Matter*. She can be reached through her website at www.pattidrapeau.com.